Gift of the
White Light

The Strange and Wonderful Story of
Annette Martin, Psychic

May the White Light be with you.

Annette Martin

Gift *of the* White Light

The Strange and Wonderful Story of Annette Martin, Psychic

A Biography by

James N. Frey

Sanger, California

Printed in the United States of America.

Published by
Quill Driver Books/Word Dancer Press, Inc.,
1254 Commerce Way, Sanger, CA 93657
559-876-2170 / 800-497-4909
QuillDriverBooks.com

Word Dancer Press books may be purchased for educational, fund-raising, business or promotional use. Please contact Special Markets, Quill Driver Books/ Word Dancer Press, Inc. at the above address or phone numbers.

Quill Driver Books/Word Dancer Press Project Cadre:
Doris Hall, Christine Hernandez, David Marion, Stephen Blake Mettee,
Cassandra Williams
First Printing

ISBN 1-884956-79-3 • 978-1884956-79-9

**To order a copy of this book, please call
1-800-497-4909.**

Library of Congress Cataloging-in-Publication Data
Frey, James N.
Gift of the white light : the strange and wonderful story of Annette
Martin, psychic / by James N. Frey.
p. cm.
Includes bibliographical references.
ISBN-13: 978-1-884956-79-9 (hardcover)
ISBN-10: 1-884956-79-3 (hardcover)
1. Martin, Annette. 2. Psychics—United States—Biography. I. Title.
BF1027.M35F74 2008
133.8092—dc22
[B]
                                                          2007036665

This book is dedicated
to the memory of Edgar Cayce

Contents

A Note to the Reader

This is the only authorized biography of Annette Martin. Many of the testimonials and eyewitness accounts cited in this book have been edited for the sake of brevity, but not for content. All of the accounts are in the actual words of the witnesses. Some of their names have been withheld or changed for reasons of privacy.

Prologue

Annette will tell you that from her earliest days, when she would go to bed at night and close her eyes, she would see a powerful White Light shining over her, enveloping her, warming her. The White Light was a comfort to her, and she knew, even from a very young age, that it was a gift from God. She gradually came to know that it was her mission in this life to learn to use its awesome power to help people.

This is the story of what Annette Martin has done with the power of the White Light, and how it has impacted and transformed her life and the lives of others.

Chapter One

How I Met Annette and Thought She Was Weird

"Annette Martin is not a wannabe-psychic; she is real!"
—John Hall, morning talk host, WCIL (Southern Illinois)

"Annette Martin is funny and entertaining. She lit up the phone lines for three solid hours!"
—Mitch Oguleqicz, afternoon drive, WNNZ, Springfield, MA

"...Phone went nuts...listeners continued to call all day! Not only does Annette give great psychic readings, she also will give caring advice to your listeners!"
—Michelle McKormick, morning co-host, WMUS, Muskegon, MI

The first time I met Annette Martin was at a birthday party for a friend who was pretty weird herself. The party was held at a restaurant, Lou's Village, one Sunday evening in San Jose, California. My friend had said that a really super psychic was coming to her party and that I ought to meet her, that she was America's greatest living psychic. She said perhaps I'd seen her on "Montel Williams" or "48 Hours," one of those guest shows on TV. My friend said this psychic was the real deal: Martin had taught classes in parapsychology at the University of Hawaii and at Stanford; she had her own radio show on KGU in Hawaii; and she had been studied by a panel of medical doctors who verified her abilities. The FBI used her a couple of times, she said—once on the Patty Hearst case.

I write for a living, both fiction and nonfiction, and I am always eager to meet people who are, let us say, in odd occupations, be they chimney sweeps, corporate spies, or circus clowns. A psychic? Why not?

I had no idea at the time that the day would come when I'd be suffering from a potentially deadly disorder called sleep apnea, and Annette Martin would be instrumental in my cure. I'll tell you all about this amazing episode later in this book.

Annette, I was to discover, is more than just the run-of-the-mill psychic who can tell you you're going to meet a beautiful stranger, fall in love, and have six screaming brats all named after your dead relatives. Sure, she can do that, but she can do much more. The Gift of the White Light, you'll see, has many surprising aspects.

Having never met a psychic, I had no idea what a psychic would be like. My overactive imagination conjured up images of somebody who spoke in hushed, mysterious tones, making dire predictions of civilization's doom. I figured she'd be wearing a pointy hat and a black dress with cryptic Egyptian symbols all over it. She'd probably have a cold stare and a hatchet face, something like the Wicked Witch of the West in *The Wizard of Oz*. She'd be really weird, I figured, in speech, manner, and dress. But then I like weird people.

I thought, too, if she were a phony, I'd spot her as a phony in about two seconds flat. I've always considered myself good at spotting phonies.

Annette, it turned out, did not fulfill my expectations. She was no hatchet-faced hag. No indeed, she looked like...well, like Debbie Reynolds in her "Singing in the Rain" days. At the time I met her, Annette was, I guess, in her late forties or early fifties—she was blond and obviously bright, open, funny, outgoing. She had a quick, lilting laugh. There was a girlish, zest-for-life quality about her; she seemed unspoiled, exuberant, optimistic, like a bouncy teenager in an adult's body. I liked her enormously from the moment we were introduced. My wife did, too.

When not stuffing my mouth with birthday cake, I chatted with Annette. At my kidding questions like why she didn't just spend her days at the race track picking winners, she'd just laugh and jab me playfully in the ribs with her elbow. I guess she'd heard that sort of stuff about a million times. Annette, I soon found, is not defensive in the least about her abilities, nor is she evasive about what she does or how she does it, but she prefers in a social situation to talk about things like movies and books and travel, pretty much the same sort of things un-psychic people talk about. The really weird thing about Annette is that, except for being a psychic, she's just "regular people."

She didn't seem like a phony to me in any way. She seemed like a straightforward, honest person you could trust to hold your wallet any time.

But even then, when I first met her, I sensed there was something painful in her past, something buried deep inside that she didn't want anyone to see, and it took me a long time to dig it out. You see, the Gift of the White Light is not exactly a free gift: It has a price. But before I tell you about what it has cost Annette, you'll need to know a little bit more about her and what she's done with the Gift of the White Light.

A Display of Talent

Seeing that I was curious about her and her work, Annette asked me if I'd like to come to a meeting of the San Francisco Psychical Society the following month. She was going to give a lecture and do one of her medical readings. I said, sure. It was to be held in a lecture hall at the University of California, Berkeley, not far from my home.

I thought, well now, okay, she seems like a straight-arrow sort of person—likeable. But aren't con artists always likeable? Then I thought, hell, a sharp fellow like me, an insurance claims adjuster turned mystery writer, I'd figure out her "medical reading" racket in two minutes flat. So I went to the meeting of the San Francisco Psychical Society, thinking of it as a challenge.

The auditorium lecture hall was a large one. There were two to three hundred people in attendance, including my wife and myself, and a writer friend, Susan Edmiston, whom I had invited along. Most everyone else was either a member of the psychical society or someone who had come with a member. There were a few skeptics present, perhaps, but most of the audience, it seemed to me, were true believers.

I thought I'd see a different Annette as a performer. Well, maybe not in a pointed hat and Egyptian symbols, but at least in a serious business suit with her blond hair put up in a bun. I thought she might wear heavy-rimmed glasses and put on a serious, even stern, demeanor. I mean, wasn't this show biz?

After the audience was settled in, one of the members of the society came onstage and introduced Annette, who was dressed in a bright blue dress, the sort the mother of the bride might wear to a wedding. She seemed her chipper self, all twinkling smiles and bubbly as a school girl, just as she had been at the birthday party.

She gave a little talk about doing medical readings, how she worked with doctors who had problems diagnosing certain ailments, and so on, which was interesting, but I wanted her to get on with the show. I wanted to see something…paranormal.

I didn't have to wait long. Annette soon went to work doing her readings. For the next hour and a half or so, volunteers came up onto the stage one at a time. Annette would stand perhaps ten feet from them and open her arms out to her sides, her palms facing the person she was "reading," and then she'd close her eyes for maybe a minute. Then she would open her eyes as if she were coming awake from a trance and talk to them about what their medical problems were and what they should do about them.

Sometimes she'd advise the volunteers to continue their present course of treatment; sometimes she'd suggest they see another doctor. She would often make specific recommendations as to which doctor, dentist, or chiropractor to see.

Her dialogue with the volunteer subject would go like this:

"You have been having terrible headaches and have been taking a lot of pain pills…"

Sometimes the person would nod or say yes, but often would just remain still and mute. It didn't matter. Annette would just go on with things like: "But the problem is not with your head. You have a neck problem…You need to see a chiropractor, a Dr. So-and-so…"

The odd thing about the demonstration was that no one said, "No, my problem is not headaches—it's my foot." No disagreements whatever. She told one man the reason he was feeling weak, she was sorry to say, was that he had testicular cancer and that he should go to the hospital immediately—it was spreading.

Annette does not back away from what she sees. What she sees, she reveals. She is straightforward as an arrow.

Whatever problem these volunteer subjects had, she seemed to know about it. I figured, oh, the psychical society told her what the problems were before the subjects came on stage and she has a phenomenal memory and could place the ailment with the person's face.

I asked Annette about this after the session. She said she didn't know these people at all, and no one told her what their problems were. I asked her how she knew all these doctors she referred people to. She just shrugged.

Come on, I repeated, how did she know? Had she memorized the medical yellow pages?

The names just came to her. She didn't know any of them, she said, amused by my skepticism.

I insisted that she must have a hidden microphone in her ear. She smiled patiently. I asked her if the CIA was helping her. "Must be it," she said in a burst of laughter.

I asked her if anyone checked with these people later to see if what she told them was right. She said she didn't know. She'd been tested for accuracy by panels of doctors and felt no need to do follow-ups. She said she had file drawers full of testimonials from people she's helped. That's what counts to her. Helping people.

Both my wife and I were impressed by Annette that night. She was either a truly great medical intuitive or she was an extremely clever charlatan. In either case we had witnessed an amazing performance.

My friend Susan Edmiston remained skeptical. She thought Annette was a great showman, but—psychic power? She shook her head; she didn't believe it. Susan is a career journalist and big-time magazine writer and a former editor for *Glamour* magazine. As hardheaded as an anvil.

Nevertheless, Annette invited Susan along with her on a trip she was about to take. It seems one Captain Wolverton of the Cascade County Sheriff's Office in Great Falls, Montana, was about to retire and he had a thirty-five-year-old unsolved murder case and wanted Annette to come and help him solve it.

Susan contacted *Cosmopolitan* magazine and scored an assignment to go along and write an article about Annette's work.

Susan and Annette met at the San Francisco airport, Susan told me later, and one of the first things Annette said was that she, Susan, should check with her doctor because she was in need of hormone treatments. Susan later did get some tests done, and yes, she needed hormone treatments. Susan, always the skeptic, said, "Well, but you could say that about any woman of a certain age and you'd often be right." She said she thought Annette was probably tipped off by her pale coloration or low energy or something and there was nothing psychic about it.

And with that attitude, off she went to Montana to witness Annette at work.

Susan was then in her late forties, a pert, comely blonde with a strong, analytical mind and a prodigious memory—coupled with an ironic sense of humor. It's the way you get when you work in New York City high-rises for longer than two weeks, and she'd worked in them for twenty years. In addition, she had a reporter's sharp eye that could spot a dust ball on a crowded dance floor.

Annette and Susan flew from San Francisco to Salt Lake City, then caught a ninety-five-minute flight to Great Falls on a commuter airline. They arrived in the crisp coolness of an autumn evening.

Great Falls is in north-central Montana. "Big Sky" country so-called, where the chamber of commerce boasts that visitors can walk in the footsteps of Lewis and Clark, visit the Ulm Pishkun Buffalo Jump Education Center and the C. M. Russell Museum of Western Art, and picnic in several beautiful city parks.

A "buffalo jump" sounds like it might be a festive occasion, but it's not. Native Americans killed buffalo there by stampeding them off the cliff.

Great Falls had a population of about 55,000 at the time. The city had been named after the thundering, magnificent falls in the nearby Missouri River. The city sits in a valley surrounded by the stark, granite peaks of the Highwood and Little Belt Mountains. It's a working-class town. People wear jeans and flannel shirts and cowboy hats and boots, and most of them shop at Wal-Mart. You see a lot of pickup trucks, older ones and newer ones, all covered with dust and dirt. The town wasn't going broke, but it wasn't all that prosperous either.

The vast, open spaces around Great Falls are a sportsman's paradise. Hunters from as far away as Germany flew in to hunt deer. Folks there would tell you the rivers were so full of trout you could walk from bank to bank on their backs without getting your toes wet.

Great Falls exhibited a strong sense of patriotism and American flags were present on houses and businesses all over the place. High school football and church potlucks attracted good crowds.

The one-runway Great Falls International Airport was three miles from town. When Annette and Susan arrived, they were met by Captain Wolverton. He was fifty-two at the time. Susan would later describe him in the *Cosmopolitan* article as "a slim, rangy man with a fine-boned nose and a beard flecked with red." Annette felt comfortable with him, as if she were meeting an old friend, she told me. Despite his rather raw-boned, outdoorsman appearance, Annette had a strong sense that he was a deep thinker with wide interests. She described him as an "outdoorsy Renaissance man." They drove into town chatting, looking at the city. Then, without warning, Annette started getting intense psychic vibes.

"Stop!" she shouted.

Captain Wolverton pulled over.

They were in a pleasant neighborhood of tree-lined streets with well-kept, but older homes. There were bikes on porches, dogs running loose, kids playing in yards.

Annette, flushed, pointed to a large, stately Victorian. "Something horrible happened there—a horrible murder! A man was killed—shot!"

Susan was taken aback. Annette was visibly shaken; sweat beaded on her palms.

Captain Wolverton remained calm. "This house is known as 'the castle,'" he said. "Two men lived in this house and one of them disappeared in 1981; we finally found him buried in the basement, with a shot gun wound to the head. We found him eight years after his suspected killer died of natural causes."

Annette breathed a sigh of relief.

Captain Wolverton went on: "Well, that's certainly a hit, a great way to start out, Annette."

Susan remained skeptical. Annette must have read about this case, she told me later, or maybe the cops had told her about it when they'd chatted on the phone before she and Annette arrived.

Annette, as usual, just chuckled when I told her what Susan surmised about this episode.

The next day, Annette would give her an even greater demonstration of her talents.

The Cottonwood Case

The crime that Annette had come to help the investigators solve involved a lovers' lane murder called the "Cottonwood case," named for a grove of cottonwood trees that stood on the banks of the Sun River, where Patti Kalitzke, sixteen, and Lloyd Duane Bogle, eighteen, were murdered during the late-night hours of January 2, 1956.

In Captain Wolverton's spacious office, painted institutional light green, Annette got out her pencil and notepad and steadied herself to go to work. The captain had a large, oak desk strewn with crime-scene photos and evidence.

Annette (right), police Captian Keith Wolverton (left), and author Ray Worring (center).

Present with Annette were astenographer (who produced the transcript this account is taken from); Susan, who also took notes; Captain Wolverton; Detective Ken Anderson; and Private Investigator Ray Worring, author (with Whitney S. Hibbard) of *Psychic Criminology*. Ray Worring had brought Captain Wolverton and Annette together as part of his continuing research. (Later, Annette would do a medical reading for Ray Worring that would save his life. The details can be found in Chapter seven).

Captain Wolverton asked Annette if she needed the dozens of photos they had.

"I only need one or two of them. One of each of the victims."

"Maybe I should break down the scenario for you," Captain Wolverton said, showing Annette the crime scene photos. "This is seven miles north of Great Falls. This is an old road, not used much." Pointing to a spot beside a cottonwood tree, he said: "This is where the girl was shot, by the tree...This is where the car was parked, right here." Patti's body was found elsewhere.

Susan asked to see the photos.

Annette wondered if they had any physical evidence she could lay her hands on. Captain Wolverton went out of the room to get the evidence pack.

"The only thing I get squeamish about are shoes," Annette said to Susan.

"What?" Susan asked.

"Shoes. I get squeamish about shoes; I don't know why."

The private eye and the detective chuckled.

Captain Wolverton returned with the evidence pack. He produced an old, faded, dirty, bloodstained dress and coat.

"Oh, my God," Susan said.

Annette put the dress and coat in her lap and held them for a few minutes. "The energy is still there," she said. She closed her eyes.

Annette let herself slip into a sort of trance, entering into the mind of victim Patti Kalitzke.

Annette described Patti as adventurous and in love with the boy she was with, Lloyd Bogle. There was a lot of "heat" coming off Patti, she said. Patti was feeling sad and guilty. "She feels bad," Annette said.

At the time of the murder, Annette went on, Patti was feeling bad because Lloyd was upset with her and they stopped on the side of the road to talk things over. Annette closed her eyes: "Yes," she went on, "She is crying...He's holding her and she's crying." The captain asked if they were having intercourse. "Yes," Annette said, "and she didn't want to do it. He feels so poor. I feel her family is poor. Is that true?"

Captain Wolverton said, "Not a real wealthy family. Middle class."

"Her dress feels cotton...light-colored on top. In the summertime she would run around barefoot a lot. Kind of a child who was open and free..."

"Free spirit?" the captain said.

"Yes, free spirit in her personality. Open to adventure, open to getting herself involved in situations that she was extremely naive about. Naive about the world, naive about life. She'd say, 'I don't understand; I don't know why people do things like that, why they say things like that'...referring to dirty things said to her." She was, Annette said, a real innocent.

Annette described the scene: The big, dark-blue car (actually a '52 Dodge), the bushes, the grove of barren cottonwood trees, the young couple arguing, the patches of snow on the ground. Then Annette "saw" their attacker, a "scruffy-looking drifter," she said. He had facial hair on his chin and cheeks, and he had high cheek bones. She described him as having thin lips and a wide nose and a large area between his nose and mouth. She added more details—he had an odor and he had fungus on his feet—and then she slipped into his mind. She said he felt desperate and unclean, trapped. Crazed.

She said the girl sensed his presence and felt scared. Annette started to shiver. "He's killed before," she said. "He sees someone else when he kills—someone named 'Mary Ann,' who rejected him." She said he "wanted to erase this memory of Mary Ann and that's why he kills."

Annette saw Patti beg for her life, saying she had done nothing to him, but this only inflamed him. She saw that he had noticed Patti and Lloyd together in town, at a restaurant or pub, with other people, and thought that Patti was "Mary Ann" and that's why he had followed them out to the lovers' lane. He jerked her out of the car and bashed her head with the butt of his gun. Lloyd came to her aid and the killer pistol-whipped him into unconsciousness, then, screaming obscenities, he dragged Patti to a tree and banged her head against it, clawing her as if he were trying to destroy her.

As they both lay unconscious, he tied their hands behind their backs. The autopsy proved Annette correct: Both victims had been beaten into unconsciousness and had their hands tied behind their backs.

Tears were streaking Annette's flushed face; she was shaking all over. But she went on. "She's gone. He killed her. And then he goes over and shoots Lloyd."

She added that she saw the killer dump Patti's body into a ravine on a country road north of Great Falls—exactly where it was found five miles north of the city. Annette kept saying she saw the number five in her vision.

Annette took a break to collect herself. Experiencing the traumas of horrible murders is but part of the price Annette pays for the Gift. Psychic Sylvia Browne believes psychics must suffer in order to have greater empathy with the human community. Maybe so. In these types of sessions, Annette suffers much pain.

When Annette resumed, she said that the killer was a mechanic and also knew farming, that he seemed mild-mannered, that he drifted from place to place, and that he had killed others following the same pattern. She added that he was now, thirty-five years later, in poor health, his mind confused and warped, and he had little desire to stay alive.

The captain then gave Annette a few dozen pictures of suspects. She picked out Robert Coxe. "That's him," she said firmly. "He's your killer!"

It turned out that the man Annette picked was a drifter, a mechanic who sometimes worked on farms. But his wife's name was "Elsie," not "Mary Ann."

Annette just shrugged. Oh, well...

Later, Annette, Susan, Captain Wolverton, and Ray Worring went out for dinner and a few drinks. When they arrived back at the Holiday Inn where Annette and Susan were staying, they found Detective Anderson waiting for them in the parking lot, grinning from ear to ear.

"Guess what?" he said. "After Annette's reading, I checked with one of Coxe's ex-girlfriends. His first wife was named Mary Ann Gallipan! She married him when she was nineteen. A year or so later, in 1952, she ditched him for another man. Coxe told the girlfriend that he had found Mary Ann necking in a car with another man."

Everyone congratulated Annette.

The Great Falls Sheriff's Office tracked down Coxe and found him in prison in California: He was a patient in the prison hospital. He had been incarcerated for a lovers' lane murder in California! Just as Annette had said, he was terribly ill—with a failing heart and tuberculosis.

Later, when Captain Wolverton interviewed him in his cell, Coxe hinted he may have been guilty of murdering Patti Kalitzke and Lloyd Duane Bogle on January 2, 1956, but he would not make a formal confession. So even though the Cottonwood case was never officially closed, for Captain Keith Wolverton it had been laid to rest.

Susan, even though she remained skeptical (in her words, "professionally detached"), wrote a wonderful article for *Cosmopolitan* magazine. She thought Annette might have obtained details about the case some other way. In what way, she didn't know.

After the article was published, two witnesses came forward. One said he saw Coxe buying ammunition for a .45—the same caliber as the murder weapon—a day or two before the murder. Later, the witness claimed he had seen what might have been blood on Coxe's clothes. The second witness said that Coxe told him on the day of the murders, "If Patti don't want to be with me, she's not going to be with nobody, especially that propeller head."

Long afterwards, Annette received some news about the Cottonwood case from Captain Wolverton, who was by then long retired, but was still in touch with the active command of the Great Falls Sheriff's Office. New technology had been applied to the case and they had taken a sample of DNA from semen found on Patti Kalitzke's clothing. Annette was delighted—this would be scientific proof that she had been right.

When next she heard from Captain Wolverton, however, there was bad news. The DNA in the sample did not match Coxe's.

Annette was at first distressed to hear this, but when we looked back at the transcript of the session she had on the case, we found nowhere in it that she had suggested that Coxe had had sex with Patti or that he had masturbated on her.

Both Annette and Captain Wolverton remain convinced that Coxe was the killer.

Chapter Two

The Power of the White Light

Annette's gifts as a psychic counselor have guided my life and professional work with devastating precision and clarity. She is undoubtedly on the forefront of her profession.
—Dyveke Spino, author of *New Age Training for Fitness and Health*, and founder of Esalen Sports Center.

Annette has collected mountainous stacks of testimonials, press clippings, and other memorabilia over the years. She asked me if I thought she had enough material for a book. She had file drawers crammed with stuff, she said. I took a look and told her I thought she had material for ten books.

Some of the testimonials are included at the beginning of chapters. I've selected a representative sample of the many hundreds, if not thousands, that Annette has in her files.

The following are a representative sample of these testimonials:

...A neighbor invited me to the University Women's Club for a luncheon, where a well-known psychic (not Annette) was scheduled to speak and she thought it would be interesting... The large convention room was filled; I had no idea that people were so interested in psychics. As soon as the main course was finished, a very tall, heavyset woman was introduced as our psychic for the day. She certainly matched all my expectations of what a psychic looks like. She was, let us say, a little witchy looking! But her voice and smile were lovely. I listened intently as she spoke about psychic energy, how it worked and how we can use it for ourselves. Everyone

seemed excited about the process when she stopped and began to point at different people from the audience, giving quick readings on their lives...I stood up and started to move towards the speaker when I heard a woman's voice say to me, 'Can I speak to you for a moment?' I turned and there was this very attractive blond woman sitting across from me. She looked so calm and loving I couldn't help but walk over to her.

She said, "I have been picking some things up about you and would like to verify them."

This really intrigued me and I quickly sat down in the empty chair next to her. She introduced herself as Annette Martin and added that she, too, was a professional psychic. Annette looked me in the eye and began to speak in a clear, loving, caring voice: "You need to see a doctor right away as I see pains that you are experiencing in your uterus and the surrounding area. There is an infection in the tubes and it should be looked at very soon."

My mouth fell open, how did she know this? I had never met this woman in my life. I gathered myself together and replied, "Yes, I am experiencing some pain but have been ignoring it."

"I am sorry to blurt out this information to you but I have been tuning into you since the luncheon started and I just had to tell you. My rules are that I never do this, but there must be a reason for it, so please forgive me if I have disturbed you."

The very next day I made an appointment to see a gynecologist in San Francisco and he verified Annette Martin's diagnosis! He gave me antibiotics and said, "I am awfully glad that you came in when you did because we could have had a very serious problem here and it could have meant a hysterectomy."

Whew! I just couldn't believe it! Annette is truly fantastic!

—June Rucker

That's how Annette came to meet June Rucker. And wanting to help Annette help other people, June Rucker began serving, without pay, as Annette's secretary.

Okay, in case you think only ignorant, superstitious people might seek Annette's services, read on. The next testimonial is from an M.D.:

...I awoke one morning with an excruciating headache which was constant, boring, and was postorbital and inter-temporal in distribution. I

have never experienced a headache such as that. Aspirin, codeine, heat, position change had no effect. There was no letup day or night; it was almost unbearable. On the 3rd day, about 11:00 A.M., on a whim, I consulted Annette Martin, who I was observing doing a medical reading with a colleague that day. She said that the source of my pain was the upper neck in the region of the 2nd or 3rd vertebrae, and she recommended a chiropractor.

When asked which one, she said, "Frank Caldwell in Sausalito."

"Do you know him?" I asked.

"No, I've never heard of him, the name just came to me," she responded.

There was a Dr. Frank Caldwell in Sausalito, and one hour after the cervical adjustment I was completely free of the headache. There has been no recurrence.

—Jerome Littell, M.D.

The following is typical of the reports from Annette's clients:

I had my first psychic reading by Annette Martin on November 21, 1978. I came to her because I had read an article in the San Francisco Chronicle, *which stated that she did medical diagnosing for a doctor.*

I just asked Annette to tune into me and tell me if she picked up any medical problems. Annette went straight to my abdominal area and told me that my intestinal track and uterus had problems. I knew that I had intestinal problems, but I was unaware of anything wrong with my uterus. She told me that I had a fibroid tumor of the uterus and told me to go and see my gynecologist.

I went to my gynecologist who at that time was Dr. Rafael Devaliay. He examined me without my telling him what Mrs. Martin had said. He found a fibroid tumor, I think about five centimeters in size, on my uterus.

My second reading by Annette Martin was on October 8, 1979. I sought her assistance again because I had been told in 1964–1965 that one of my legs was shorter than the other and had been wearing a lift in my shoe for about fourteen years and I had been having my back adjusted by a chiropractor according to the diagnosis that one leg was shorter than the other. At that point in 1979, my back had really been bothering me and the lift had always been annoying.

I asked Mrs. Martin if my legs were really uneven. She said, "No, and you must change chiropractors."

So, I did. A Dr. J. J. Maniscalco examined me, said my legs were even, made a simple adjustment on my back and I haven't worn a lift since and haven't had any apparent problems because of this. Also during the same reading in 1979, Annette told me that I was very low in the mineral potassium and that my mineral content in general vacillated greatly. I had a hair mineral analysis done shortly after the reading and the results do show that my body is low in potassium as well as almost all other minerals.

—Patricia Klahn

Some of the letters Annette has received refer to long-standing problems that modern medicine has not been able to cure. Here's an example:

In January 1977, I went to Annette Martin's office for a reading. I've suffered from bleeding gums since I was fourteen years old. Bleeding would occur each time I brushed my teeth. My gums would be swollen most times...Eventually I asked a dentist about this problem. As time passed, many other dentists had a chance to express their opinions. Their opinions varied from my having to learn how to properly brush my teeth to a possible case of pyorrhea. They confessed not knowing what to do about it. From that time on I had to live with my problem.

Then last January I came to Annette with this problem. I did not tell Annette what the problem was, but she closed her eyes and immediately saw my gums! Annette told me it was something in the blood that caused the problem, especially in times of tension. It was recommended that I buy fresh spearmint leaves, soak the leaves in hot water for five minutes, let the mixture cool, and then rinse my mouth for five to ten minutes each time I brushed my teeth. The first two weeks I noticed no change. Starting the third week, however, the swelling began to subside and the lesions began to heal. The color of the gums began to change from a sick bluish color to a healthy pink. I continued this treatment for four months. My gums are now completely healed!

This was a twenty-three-year-old gum condition which all dentists failed to cure, but my favorite psychic, Annette Martin, cured me in one reading!

—Miriam Levy

Some of the cases addressed to Ms. Martin are more serious than just bleeding gums. Here's a testimonial by an accident victim who sought Annette's help:

A yellow station wagon pressed against the left side of my body as I walked across the crosswalk in the Bullock's parking garage. I was thrown forward off the car and bounced off the curb. When I regained consciousness, four people were moving me by pulling on all four of my limbs. Within weeks I was totally disabled and in so much pain there were not enough painkillers to help. Four, five, six months went by and I was getting worse. My physical therapist was even scared for my life. A visit from my friend alarmed by my failing condition told me about Annette Martin, an unusual psychic who worked with doctors on hard-to-diagnose cases. So with nothing to lose, I called for an appointment.

Sitting across from this beautiful woman with smiling eyes, I could only dare to hope that she might be able to help me. She dropped into a trance, but she quickly popped out of it stating, "My God, woman, you are in a lot of pain!" I thought to myself, "So tell me something I don't know!" She did so for the next hour.

She detailed exactly what parts of my spine were damaged, what vertebras were out, what muscles were injured, and what body functions that had shut down. The worse misalignment she stated was, "a twenty-six-degree maladjustment that is at L 5, in the lower back." Annette went on, "I want you to see a Dr. Robert Culver, in Los Altos. He is a chiropractor that has remarkable healing hands. I know that he will heal you and you will be good as new." For the first time, I felt hopeful.

After Dr. Robert Culver's exam, I was amazed at how Annette had pinpointed every major problem in my muscles and spine. Right down to the exactness of the degree in which the spine was maladjusted.

It took Dr. Robert Culver two full years to rebuild my body. Understand that I could not walk or open a car door on my own. The first month I was at Dr. Culver's office five days a week, three to five hours a day. As I started to show signs of improvement, people were in awe to see the depth of recovering that took place. In two years, due to the accurate diagnosis and guidance by Annette Martin, my body was restored to health and beauty once again. I will always be grateful to this beautiful lady for saving my life.

You are an incredible woman with an outrageous talent! Keep up the good work! I hope you are half as helpful to the others that you see as you are to me. You are a dear soul and a good friend. God bless you...
— Sidney Chase

The last testimonial is a transcript from the testimony given on the air by TV news anchor Jerry Jensen, at KGO in San Francisco.

KGO was doing a special series on psychics. When Annette arrived, Mr. Jensen asked her to do a reading for him—on the air. She said that often what she had to say was personal and it would be better if she did her reading in private. He agreed. The following is Jerry Jensen's on-the-air report of that private reading:

You won't believe this because I can hardly believe the things that Annette Martin told me in a reading less than forty minutes ago. We asked her to do it over the air and she refused. Boy, am I glad she refused! When she said that she gets personal, believe me folks, she does!

She started out telling me that I had an infection in my right ear. My mouth fell open on that, because I am still taking antibiotics for an ear infection in my right ear! Then she continues with, there is a little problem with the heart; it keeps missing a beat now and then. I told her she was right again. That was diagnosed by my doctor three years ago. Then she told me about the time when I was in high school, someone punched me in the stomach and I doubled over in pain.

Folks, this is correct. I had to go to the emergency room because the punch was so bad. Annette went on from there: "Well, there are little granules in the urine, looks like there is a cystitis condition there. But no need to worry. It's chronic, but will not develop into anything major."

"Whew! Thank goodness for that," I replied. "You get an A+ on that one, because I definitely have a cystitis condition, which has been with me for a long time, but the doctor assured me it would not get any worse if we keep tabs on it. Doctor labeled it 'Granules Case' in the urine."

The next thing I knew she was rubbing her knee like crazy with a pained look on her face. She asked me if I had ever hurt my knee. She said that the knee has a white line going through it. My eyes widened and I replied, "At twenty-two years of age, I ran a sledge pin right through my knee cap and it was pinned in there till the doctors removed it!"

The last and final blow came when she said, "There is this shadow in between your big toe and second toe. Something is wrong there. I can't see exactly what it is but it appears as a shadow." That was it! "That's my athlete's foot," I shouted. "Not even my wife knows about that!"

Impressive testimonials, to be sure. Out of curiosity, I asked Annette if she had ever been tested in a scientific laboratory. She said she had been tested by Professor Jeffrey Smith at Stanford, who came to her office. What follows is a transcript of the recording made of the session:

DR. S.: This is a copy of a painting and it's rolled up in black velvet cloth so that there is no way that you can see into it. And perhaps if you feel like it, you can give us any impressions that you have.

ANNETTE: As soon as you handed it to me I see the color of blue. A very pretty color of blue.

DR. S.: Yes.

ANNETTE: [*sigh*] It's a boy; I see a boy. This is a print, huh?

DR. S.: Yes.

ANNETTE: The picture is in the inside and there is much space all around the edges. [*Annette made a sign of about an inch and a half with her fingers*]. It's kind of off-white, cream color.

DR. S.: The shape is exactly as you described it.

ANNETTE: I am seeing different shades of blue. Very beautiful blue in there. I see a boy.

DR. S.: Describe the boy; tell us what he is doing.

ANNETTE: It looks like he is standing there and you know, he looks like he has short pants on. Funny pants, Blue Boy.

DR. S.: You are doing very well! Tell us about the boy; what is he doing?

ANNETTE: Is there a dog?

DR. S.: Yes.

ANNETTE: I see ruffles in the shirt. Are there small ruffles, kind of like this [indicating ruffles on her blouse]?

DR. S.: I don't know. Tell us about the dog or any other animals you see.

ANNETTE: The dog—it looks like it has long hair. The dog is sitting. Looks like a long nose, like an Afghan dog. Long hair and a long nose. I am seeing him sitting very proud.

DR. S.: What else do you see in the picture?

ANNETTE: Looks like a scene in the distance. Pastel colors. Like a mountain. Looks like the outside, for sure.

DR. S.: It is an outside scene. Tell us more about the scene.

ANNETTE: Some of the mountains are shaped like this, in the background. Yellow something around. Looks like a house in the distance. Not sure, not sure.

DR. S.: What's the boy doing; can you see?

ANNETTE: He is just standing there.

DR. S.: That's exactly right! What else?

ANNETTE: Hair—hair, it looks brown. Must be kind of curly.

DR. S.: What's he doing standing there?

ANNETTE: Ah, there's a connection to the dog, maybe because of love.

DR. S.: What mood does the boy have; what is his mood?

ANNETTE: Ah, pensive. I don't see much expression in his face.

DR. S.: You're right! How then is he expressing himself?

ANNETTE: Not happy—sad. It looks like he is staring. I get a pensive, longing feeling. I see a shirt to the waist line and there seems to be a gap and it looks like the shirttail is coming out. Like a vest or a jacket. Blue. And the pants, like pantaloons. Yeah, maybe like this. A little above the ankle.

DR. S.: Yes. Now what position are his arms and legs in?

ANNETTE: He seems like he's on one foot? One knee seems to be in front. The right leg.

DR. S.: Yes, yes. Now put your arms the way the boy's are.

ANNETTE: Let me see—the hands are open, but I don't know what they are doing. There is something rectangular, I think, in the upper right of the painting, but I can't make out what it is.

DR. S.: What part of the world is this scene in?

ANNETTE: Not American. I am getting French. I am getting countryside. Dusty, rural.

DR. S.: Yes, correct on the countryside. On French, I would have to say in a way, yes, and in a way, no. The place itself is not in France.

ANNETTE: Now I am seeing a woman with a long dress. Long full skirt, from the waist. I can see the big pleat coming down.

DR. S.: Yes, that's true. Can you see who painted the painting?

ANNETTE: I see a beret; he wore a beret, a long brush, long hair. R. R. The painter was French.

DR. S.: Yes, he was French, but not Renoir. He followed Renoir and was greatly influenced by him. But it is very different from Renoir.

ANNETTE: I see him painting with long brushes. Very articulate, a perfectionist. His hands, oh, the artist hands. Very expressive. He used his hands like this [dabbing]. There is a large area between the first finger and the thumb. Unusual, because a person who has a large area there is very earthy and likes the earth. He had these magnificent hands. The painter had dark hair.

DR. S.: He did and he was actually very earthy. His hair was dark.

ANNETTE: I feel the helplessness in this boy, in the painting. Outstretched, pleading. Help, help me!

DR. S.: You have your arms out in front of you; is that where they are?

ANNETTE: Yes, this is what I feel he is doing and saying, help, almost like a begging, a pleading.

DR. S.: That's absolutely correct! Now let's look up to the right and see what that mysterious object is that you saw earlier.

ANNETTE: I get the feeling of a cage.

DR. S.: What color do you get?

ANNETTE: Yellowish brown. I don't like what I see. Wait a minute. I see what looks like bars, bamboo bars. I don't like it. Jail, a confining place. He is a waif. He is a beggar. He is the child; I don't see parents. An orphan, all alone.

DR. S.: You're right! Then who can he look to?

ANNETTE: He is begging to people, to give him some money, to eat, a beggar. Begging, begging.

DR. S.: Excellent, Annette! As you look at the painting you will see that you were approximately 90 percent accurate...

I asked Annette what painting it was, and she didn't know. He was doing the test, after all. I think we can accept his judgment that she was 90 percent accurate.

Annette Does a Reading for Me

Okay, I was impressed by the massive amounts of evidence, but I was still skeptical. I wanted to put Annette to the test. I picked out a photo of a woman I knew would be a stranger to Annette. I had her do a reading of this woman from the photo only, and do it on the phone so I'd know she wasn't reading my facial expressions. I mailed her the photo.

All she asked was where she lived (Syracuse, New York) and her name (withheld). Let's call her Jane.

The photo shows a woman dressed in a tee shirt and wearing glasses. She's sitting at a table with some half-filled glasses and empty bottles. At her hand is a bottle of water; she's smiling amicably at the camera. The photo was obviously taken at an informal social gathering; there are some other people in the background chatting with each other, drinks in their hands.

I told her nothing else. Absolutely nothing.

Over the phone, I heard her take three deep breaths. The following is what she told me:

—that Jane is extremely smart, perhaps even a genius. (True.)

—that Jane has a lot of masculine energy, in fact, she has almost no female energy. (Most people who know her would say that.) So far, I was impressed because she certainly looks feminine enough in the photo.

—that Jane is a writer of fiction. (True.)

—that her stories lack emotion. (True.)

—that she over-analyzes. She's calculating in life and in her fiction. (True.)

—that she's writing about and studying the Old West and wagon trains moving west, and that she has a deep interest in history and that this interest may be inspired by something she did in a past life. (She does have a deep interest in history.) At the time of Annette's reading, I knew she was writing mysteries, but I checked with people who are still in touch with her and they said she was writing about the Old West. So Annette was not reading my mind; she knew things I did not know.

—that she's an engineer of some kind. (False. She's not an engineer, but her work is highly technical and involves computers and other high-tech devices in the medical area.)

—that she has a lot of anger and was abused as a child. (True. I know for certain she was psychologically abused.)

—that she was sexually abused as a child. (I don't know for sure, but I always suspected she was.)

—that she needs a lot of counseling but would never get it. (True.)

—that she has a lot of followers who don't dare argue with her. (Very true. I thought this was amazing.)

—that she sometimes slams the door on a relationship right out of the blue. (True.)

And then Annette said: "Oh my God, she did it to you, didn't she?" (True.)

—that she's a secret alcoholic. (Possibly true. Many people who know her suspect it. She certainly spends a lot of time in wine shops.)

—that she has a lot of people mad at her. (True.)

And then Annette told me some medical things I had no way of knowing. That her molars are bad and are pumping poison into her system. That she snacks on salty stuff and so has edema. She also said she had a weak pancreas and would have trouble with that organ in the years to come.

And that she is making big plans for something, but Annette didn't know what. I had no way of knowing if she were right about this at the time of the reading, but since then it has proved to be correct.

A very remarkable reading, considering that Annette had been given no information whatsoever.

I was sold. The next day I told her I wanted to write this biography.

Chapter Three

The Adventures
of a Young Psychic

Working with Annette on several occasions, I have gained important insights that have facilitated personal and artistic growth. Her readings are highly accurate, and have included specific suggestions that I have already included in my life to assist me in staying in tune.
—Steven Halpern, Ph.D., composer, producer, author

A caller on KGU Talk Radio asked Annette Martin if she could see who was going to win the game between the Miami Dolphins and the New York Jets to be played the next day in the Orange Bowl.

Annette replied, "I don't do numbers very well, but I will try to see something. I don't see any score the first half and then I see a double digit number for Miami like a 1 and a 4 and then one other number. Maybe a 9 or a 0?"

Neither team scored in the first half; the final score was Miami 14, Jets 0.

The game was played on January 23, 1983.

I was curious about how Annette had acquired her talent. Her quick answer is "It's in the genes," and it's true: Psychic ability seems to run in families. In Annette's case, both sides of her family had it, so she got what she calls a "double whammy." Her grandmother on her mother's side lived in San Francisco, and she drew large crowds doing card readings for people as entertainment at a local restaurant one night a week for many years, using an ordinary deck of cards. How she did this trick, Annette says, was that she was in fact an amazingly talented clairvoyant and could see people's past and future lives as soon as she met them.

On Annette's father's side, her grandmother's sister, Marie, was a French nun who in 1894 foretold the assassination of French President Carnot "with a bouquet of flowers," and indeed he was killed that year by a man who hid his dagger in a floral bouquet. Years later she had a vision of the German invaders in World War I raping and murdering and was able to give warning to her fellow sisters, who managed to narrowly escape from their convent. Other nunneries were not so lucky.

Annette's mother's youngest sister Floydee, who lived in San Francisco, could see ghosts, but it scared her half to death, so she did what many psychics do: She turned off her ability. Annette's cousin Candy apparently inherited the ghost-seeing ability. One night she screamed at them to get away from her; she wanted no more dead people in her room. They stopped coming.

Another reason to believe the ability is genetic, Annette says, is that it often manifests itself early in life. Since I started working on this book, I've done some reading about psychics and found they often report psychic experiences in childhood.

Annette (left) at 16 months with her maternal grandmother and year-old cousin, Harvey.

Sylvia Browne, in *Adventures of a Psychic* (1990), reported having psychic experiences as long as she could remember. Psychic medium John Edwards, who has had his own TV show, "Crossing Over," is reported to have exhibited psychic abilities very young—his family knew he was "special" almost from birth. Emanuel Swedenborg, the eighteenth-century psychic and medium often called the "founder of modern spiritualism," and who "saw" Stockholm burning from Gothenburg 300 miles away, showed psychic abilities while still a toddler. Psychic and medium James Van Praagh, now a TV personality and best-selling author, had an encounter at eight years old with the "Hand of God," when it appeared through the ceiling of his room, emitting radiant beams of light.

Annette has been seeing what she calls the "White Light" at bedtime from an early age, but when she was a child, she kept it a secret rather than have people think she was "different." This is a common pattern with psychic children; they often hide their abilities. Psychic children who don't hide these talents frequently display remarkable abilities at an early age.

It seems that there are people who can intuitively detect the Gift in others. One of Annette's earliest memories is an encounter with such an intuitive.

Annette's family owned a small antique shop on Army Street in San Francisco. When Annette was a baby, her mother used to bring her along while she was running the store. One day, two nuns in black habits came in to admire the antiques and curios in the shop. They noticed Annette in her baby buggy. One of the nuns took one look at Annette and was taken aback. She turned to Annette's mother and asked if she could pick up the baby. Her mother nodded.

The nun lifted Annette high over her head, then slowly put her down.

"This child," she said softly, "is very special. She will be able to see things that others cannot see. Take care of her; she will help many." The two nuns slipped silently out of the store.

Annette's mother, though, probably already knew—but was not too happy about it. There are those who seem to have an almost instinctual aversion to people with the Gift; much to Annette's dismay, Annette's mother was among them.

How Annette, as a Young Girl, Was Attacked by a Mob of Other Children

Those who have an aversion to psychics often fear them.

The fear can be intense, bordering on hysteria. People hate those whom they fear. This hatred frequently to bloody violence. Psychic children are often attacked and sometimes murdered by a relative—or even a playmate—for what seems like no reason at all. In days gone by, psychic children might have been accused of witchcraft or having the "evil eye" and suffered lynching or burning at the stake.

Newspaper accounts of child murders sometimes print comments from the killers that the victims were weird or strange, or that the victims were listening in on the killers' thoughts. In court, these sorts of statements are usually attributed to the killer's psychotic paranoia, but it's possible the killer might have had an actual paranormal experience. These things are not well understood because the study of parapsychology is outside the parameters of mainstream science and therefore gets little funding.

Annette's mother may have sensed that Annette would have this special ability even before she was born. Her mother, out of fear perhaps, had not wanted Annette to be born and had unsuccessfully tried to abort her four times. Annette began paying the price for the Gift of the White Light almost from conception.

On the surface, Annette's childhood looked ideal and happy. But underneath the surface, her situation was grim. Her mother treated Annette with cold indifference, and her father, although Annette always felt he loved her deeply, was away working most of the time. He was a successful junk dealer, and during World War II he headed up what was called the San Francisco Scrap Metal Project. Scrap metal was an important source of material for the war effort. Annette felt lonely and isolated in the family.

Some of her friends, too, may have sensed something different about Annette, a situation that triggered one of those paranormal events that can happen to a psychic child.

Here is how Annette remembers it:

It was an unseasonably warm San Francisco day in December 1943, a week or so after Annette's seventh birthday. Annette loved singing, dancing, and skipping rope with her friends in front of her home on Kissling Street. She had a lovely singing voice and a natural musical ability and dreamed of one day being a singer and actress on a stage, dressed in beautiful gowns.

She lived with her parents in what was called the "South of Market" area of San Francisco, an area of warehouses and light manufacturing and working-class housing. Because of the war, San Francisco, a major West Coast port, was bustling with activity. It was the main embarkation point for service personnel and supplies going overseas to the Pacific theater of operations.

But of course, to barely seven-year-old Annette the war was remote, a dark shadow on everyday life, something people talked about, but it seemed to have no effect on her—except for the times the authorities held scary blackout drills that sent Annette's family scurrying into the basement.

Annette attended school at Notre Dame de Victoria, the Catholic French school, so she could become bilingual, but after school she played with her friends in the neighborhood. Her neighborhood was ethnically diverse: The kids were the children of Italians, Germans, Greeks, Mexicans, Filipinos, and others. Annette's mother's bloodline was Welsh and French. Her father was of Belgian and French ancestry, but he had been born in Vancouver, British Columbia, Canada.

On this particular day, Annette and her friends were playing kick-the-can in the street. Her block dead-ended at St. Joseph's Elementary School, so it was safe to play in the street. The houses were comprised mostly of what were called "row houses"—two-story flats that butted up against each other.

Kick-the-can is sort of like soccer, only a can is used instead of a ball. Any number of kids can play. That day there were perhaps a dozen, most of them older than Annette. It was the girls against the boys. They were running up and down the block, screaming and cheering joyfully, red-faced and sweating in the unseasonably warm weather, when something strange and unexpected happened—

Annette had a terrifying vision.

It hit her with shocking suddenness in the middle of the game.

She could see in her mind's eye her friends turning on her and chasing her, throwing rocks at her, trying to punch and kick her!

She stopped in her tracks. What was this? She had no idea. It was not real—it was like she was seeing a terrifying movie in her head.

She rubbed her eyes to make the vision go away. She felt a pang of guilt that she could even imagine her friends doing such a terrible thing. Her friend Pamela shook her. "What's wrong with you? What are you staring at? Come on, we have to beat the pants off these boys!"

Annette shook off her fear and went back to game, racing up and down the street amid the shouting and hollering. Her teammate Laura scored a point and the girls jumped for joy; the boys turned on them, playfully saying they were going to get them.

And then, a few minutes later, what Annette had seen in her mind began to unfold for real:

Something struck her on the back of the leg, cutting her. She ignored it. She was used to getting scraped and cut and skinning her knees playing kick-the-can on hard pavement.

Then, as she kicked the can, something struck her in the back, knocking the wind out of her. Then a rock hit her in the arm. She turned to look.

What she had seen in her terrible vision was happening for real! Her friends were attacking her, swarming over her.

Panic gripped her.

She tried to run, but she was surrounded. Her friends were closing in on her, threatening her, and they weren't joking. She had indeed entered into a nightmare. Annette screamed for help as they clutched at her. She wriggled away and broke through them and ran for her house. Something cut her arm.

Rocks and bottles showered down on her as she screamed, "Help me! Help me!"

Her own voice sounded strange to her, distant, as if it were coming through a tube.

She tripped and fell, and got up and ran again.

She reached her front stairs and managed to clamber up them, pounding on the door, screaming, sobbing.

But the door didn't open. She turned to face her attackers—a blur of angry, hateful faces. She thought they were going to kill her for certain.

A piece of wood came hurtling at her, narrowly missing her head, and bounced at her feet. Annette's mind was flooded with images of death; the scene before her seemed to go into slow motion.

Then, for the first time in her life, she heard a deep baritone voice in her head. It boomed:

"Pick up that stick!"

Annette thought for a moment the voice might belong to her father. She cried out for him to save her.

But the massive gray door to her house was still closed. Her father wasn't there—no one was there!

The voice ordered her to pick up the stick and throw it.

She stopped her sobs and picked up the stick.

In her young life she had never deliberately tried to hurt anyone. But she knew that if she didn't, she would surely die, for the kids she faced were intent on killing her.

She threw the stick as hard as she could at the face of one of her attackers, a big kid named Jos.

He screamed and fell back, blood gushing from his nose.

Even though Annette's screams had not drawn attention from any adults, oddly Jos' screams did. Suddenly the street was full of adults wanting to know what was going on. Jos' mother was comforting him and blotting the blood that ran down his nose, yelling for someone to call an ambulance.

Annette's grandmother appeared and carried her to her (the grandmother's) house next door.

The kids drifted off. Jos was taken away to receive medical care.

What sudden, strange impulse had gripped the other kids, Annette was never able to find out. Perhaps it was the same phenomenon that took over witch-burning mobs.

Strangely, the adults did not ask what had happened. Perhaps they thought the boy had been hurt playing kick-the-can. Or perhaps at some dark level of their minds, they knew what had happened and didn't wish to speak of it. In any case, Annette was hurt and confused, and the adults were not helping.

More Strange Behavior

Annette's grandmother and grandfather, "Nannie" and "Poppie," took care of Annette while her parents worked.

She had expected Nannie and Poppie to tend to her wounds and comfort her. But they didn't. They wouldn't even listen to her side of the story and kept scolding her in French—what a terrible girl Annette had been! What a horrible thing to have happen in the neighborhood. Poppie led Annette straight for what he called the "perfume room," an old-fashioned bathroom with a water tank high above the bowl, with a chain hanging down. He threw her onto the floor and locked her in.

Her grandmother pleaded with him to let her clean up Annette's wounds, but her grandfather kept shouting in French, "Let her lick her own wounds." As if she were an animal.

Annette cried, feeling helpless and delirious and terribly alone.

She yelled that she had been attacked, not the other way around, but her grandfather would not listen and would not open the door. After a couple of hours, her grandmother did prevail, and the door was opened. Annette sat in a pool of blood.

Annette managed to say, "Am I dead, Nannie? Am I in hell?"

Her grandmother cleaned her up and comforted her until her father came to take her home around six that evening.

As he was tucking her into her bed that night, Annette frantically told him what had happened, that the kids were chasing her and trying to kill her and that she'd only struck the boy in self-defense and in obedience to the voice she'd heard. She pleaded with him to believe her.

He said he did believe her about the attack, and he also told her that she had someone special looking out for her. He kissed her and tucked her in, and insisted she get some rest.

Annette stayed inside for three days at her grandmother's house, until Saturday. She was then escorted to the door and told to go outside and play with her friends. Her father assured her they would not hurt her again.

Annette was incredulous. She went outside, she remembers, trembling, terrified her friends might try to kill her again.

She found her friends waiting to play with her, even Jos, who was still wearing a bandage across his broken nose. Her father had been right: All was forgotten. They never again tried to hurt her. Nor was this strange event ever mentioned by any of them.

She never learned how her grandmother and her father knew it would be all right for her to go out that day and play with her friends. Perhaps they knew that this was a seminal event in Annette's life, and that such incidents are known to happen to psychics.

Hearing the deep baritone voice that saved her was a transitional moment for Annette, and maybe it was a necessary one. She found out she could hear the voice of someone who was looking out for her, the voice of someone she could trust.

Annette Begins to Develop Her Powers

Annette remembers the Gift coming on her gradually, mysteriously, ever stronger and stronger. Since the day the neighborhood children attacked her, the everyday world had changed into a magical world of colorful pictures of people's auras and the structures within people's bodies, and strange "whooshing" sounds that lived inside other people.

Jack Schwarz, a medical intuitive and president of the Althea Foundation that he founded in 1958, saw auras around people before he could walk. Irish psychic Eileen J. Garrett saw auras when she was a child, auras which she called "surrounds." She saw them around people, animals, and even plants before she was four.

Annette not only saw auras around people, animals, and plants, she saw them around inanimate objects. Sometimes the auras were of different colors, usually indicating something was "wrong" with them.

Luckily for Annette, some of her extended family seemed to understand what was happening.

Annette's grandmother, the one who lived next door, had a sister in France who was a Roman Catholic nun and a clairvoyant, as mentioned earlier. And Annette's father was quite intuitive, she recalls, so they did not laugh at her.

One overcast, misting day about two weeks after the incident in which the children had attacked her, Annette was walking to the store with her mother. Near the store, on a crowded sidewalk, Annette accidentally bumped into a woman in the street. At that moment she heard the same deep voice in her head that she had heard during her attack, saying that she should pay attention, that the lady had something wrong with her stomach and needed to see a doctor right away.

Seven-year-old Annette, starting to see auras.

Confused, Annette thought her mother, walking next to her, had spoken with a hushed voice. But the deep baritone voice spoke again, telling her the woman had little bad bugs in her stomach and needed to see a doctor.

Annette told her mother, who said simply that it was all right, the woman would see a doctor, and they walked on.

Then one day a few weeks later, Annette's mother was at home and received a visit from her friend, Pauline Moses. The two women drank coffee and chatted while Annette played happily with her dolls. After

Pauline Moses had gone home, Annette heard the voice in her head saying that Pauline had an infected toe, and this time, she received a vision of an infected toe with the message.

She ran to her mother and told her what she saw. Annette remembers telling her mother that Pauline's big right toe "really, really hurt." Annette's mother was a bit incredulous. "Surely, if her toe hurt, she would have said something about it. Pauline complains about everything."

But Annette persisted: The woman needed to see her doctor. Her mother finally gave in and promised to call her friend, but she didn't. The next day Pauline called her and said that after she had had tea, on the way home, her toe started hurting something awful and she was up all night in terrible pain. She went to the podiatrist and he had to take the nail off; there was a bad infection and if it hadn't been treated she could have gotten blood poisoning.

Annette's mother did not seem pleased, as if there was something bad about seeing sickness in people. So Annette did what many psychic children do: She tried her best to shut down the Gift. She looked away when she saw bad auras around people and heard noises inside them. She'd be just a normal kid, she decided.

In fact, at this time she didn't want to be called Annette any more—she wanted to be "Annie." Annie Sunshine. A happy little kid who was completely normal and wanted nothing more than to be a singer and actress.

Her mother said her name was Annette and it would always be Annette, and that was all there was to it. She never wanted to hear that name, Annie Sunshine, again. From then on, it was Annette's secret name for herself.

Annette Meets Her Spirit Guide

But she couldn't quiet her voice, not completely. A few years later, eleven-year-old Annette was praying at St. Gabriel's altar when her spirit guide visited her once more. At that time she was thinking of becoming a nun and so she did a lot of praying, asking God to show her her mission in life. A grayish-white mist started to form in front of her. Sitting back on her heels, Annette blinked and gasped: The mist was forming into the shape of a man! He was dressed only with a white loincloth wrapped around him. At first she thought it might be Jesus. He had a kind face and long, thick, wavy, dark-brown hair highlighted with red. She could not see his feet; they were hidden by the mist.

"I have been waiting for the right time to show myself," he said softly, "so you would not be frightened."

The voice! It was the same baritone voice that had told her to throw the stick!

"Who—who are you, sir?" she managed.

"My name is Camatcha," he said. "But you can call me Cama. I lived many hundreds of years ago in the Valley of the Gods, in a land far away."

Annette was shocked. The voice she'd been hearing was the voice of a ghost. She shivered. She'd seen enough cheap Hollywood horror films to know ghosts were nothing to mess with.

"I have been with you since the day you were born, and I am here to assist you in any way that I can."

"Thank you for telling me about the stick that I threw at the boy's nose," she said sheepishly. "And was that you showing me the lady's stomach, and Pauline's big right toe?"

"Yes," he said in his calm, soothing voice. "And I will continue to help you along the path of the White Light."

"Thank you, Cama. But what is the White Light? Is it the light I see just before I go to sleep? Or is it the light I see around people before I see the colors around them?"

"Yes, my child, what you see at night is the White Light. You must always keep this around yourself and you can teach others how to use it for the good of their bodies and minds. You will help many people with the White Light and you will teach many others to use it, too."

Just then there was a noise behind her. A nun had come in and was kneeling in a pew at the back of the church. When Annette looked around again, Cama was gone.

Annette Gives a Warning

Later that year, Annette's grandmother and grandfather, "Nannie" and "Poppie," received an invitation to visit Great Aunt Leontine—

Annette's grandmother's sister—in Quebec, Canada. They decided to drive and Annette was invited, too. She was thrilled—a new adventure!

It was the summer of 1948. They set off from San Francisco in Poppie's new Studebaker, planning to view the country along the way. It promised to be a hot, dusty trip.

They drove through what seemed to young Annette as endless hot deserts, over the Rocky Mountains, and across the plains. They stopped at the Great Salt Lake, saw the Mormon Temple, watched buffalo grazing in the sun. Annette was in awe. She'd never realized the country was so immense! There were summer thunderstorms in the Midwest such as she had never seen in California. They lit up the sky and peals of thunder rolled across the trackless open space. To eleven-year-old Annette, the city girl with the love of drama, this was a spectacular show.

There were no interstate highways then, and Route 40 meandered through towns and, while taking short side trips to see sights of interest, Poppie often got them lost. Once, in rural Michigan, he stopped to read a map under the dim light of the dashboard "map" light. It was a hot, clear night. Annette was half-asleep in the back seat. Suddenly the voice of Cama, her spirit guide, spoke to her:

Get away! Run! You'll be killed!

"Poppie!" she yelled in French, "We've got to get out of here!"
"Simmer down girl, we're lost," he said, fumbling with the map.
"No! We've got to go! Now!"
"Hush!" he ordered.
Cama's voice was persistent: *Get going now!*
Annette clambered over the seat to get out of the car. Her grandfather yanked her back. "I said sit!"
Annette screamed: "We've got to get out of here! We'll be killed!"
She kept struggling, trying to climb out through the window. "All right," Poppie said, cursing, and he slammed the car into gear. He hit the accelerator and the car shot forward—just as a freight train came thundering by. They had been parked on the railroad tracks!

After taking a moment to stop shaking and hug his wife and granddaughter, Poppie said:

"Any time you get one of your premonitions like that, Annette, don't hesitate to let us know."

Annette was greatly pleased. Not only had her voice saved her beloved Poppie and Nannie and herself, it was an affirmation that the voice spoke true, and indeed, it was just as her father had said—there was definitely someone watching out for her.

The Strange Thing that Happened in Quebec

Great Aunt Leontine was staying at her summer home on Lake Massawippi, a few hours outside of Montreal. It was a beautiful, forested area; the hot, gusty breezes smelled strongly of pine. Poppie drove up the gravel drive and parked in the wide driveway on the edge of a gently sloping lawn. Beyond was the large, shimmering lake surrounded by summer homes and thick forest.

Great Aunt Leontine's house stood majestically on a small rise. It was gabled in the Victorian style and had a wide, screened-in porch with half a dozen rocking chairs. Both the house and the grounds were immaculately kept.

As they came up the walk, Great Aunt Leontine's daughter, Andrea, came out to greet them. She was a short woman, in her early thirties. Her hair, Annette remembers, was cut like a man's. She had a sweet, round face, and spoke only French. She helped with their luggage and showed them in, where Aunt Leontine was waiting in the large drawing room with an enormous stone fireplace, massive mahogany tables, and overstuffed chairs. The place smelled of the cooking going on in the kitchen. Annette hoped they had lots of cookies.

Nannie had not seen her sister in years, and when they met, they hugged in a rather stiff and formal way, Nannie shedding a tear.

Great Aunt Leontine was a widow in her mid-fifties at the time. Tall, slightly bent-over, she had grayish-brown hair and wore thick glasses. Annette could see her great aunt was a rather unbending, rigid, judgmental woman and she was a little bit afraid of her.

But then Annette could see something else—her insides were grayish, her aura, dark. Her great aunt, it struck Annette, was desperately ill.

"Why are you staring at your great aunt?" Poppie wanted to know.

Annette gulped.

"What is it you are seeing?" her great aunt asked.

"I see dark shadows and spots inside you…" Annette managed. "You're very sick."

Poppie started to scold her, but Great Aunt Leontine cut him off. "It's true," she said, "I asked you to come for a visit so I could make my farewells…I'm dying."

She hugged Annette and kissed her. "My sister, Marie, who is a nun in France has the Gift, too," she said. "They say it runs in families." This was the first time Annette had heard about her other great aunt, the nun, who had the Gift of the White Light.

Annette felt sad that her great aunt was dying. She sensed her aunt had had an unhappy life and had never really felt loved. Annette was no longer afraid of her; she just felt sorry for her.

Annette and her grandparents spent a week there, taking long walks. Annette went swimming in the lake and did some rowing in a small boat. Great Aunt Leontine, who normally didn't like children, baked for Annette and sat with her and told her stories of her sister, the nun, who had the Gift. When Annette and her grandparents left, Great Aunt Leontine gave her a hug and told her to use her clairvoyance, as her great aunt had done, to serve others.

She did not tell her great aunt she wanted to be a singer and actress; she certainly wasn't going to be a clairvoyant, whatever that was.

Annette says that after this trip, when they got home, her grandfather definitely treated her differently, with far more affection. He would play the piano and sing to her for hours, as if, Annette says, "he was trying to make someone very, very special, very, very happy."

Chapter Four

Annette as
Singer and Psychic

Dear Annette:

Your reading was very interesting and I enjoyed it very much. You held my mother's photo and told me that her kidneys were very bad, especially the left kidney, and she needed to see a specialist. I phoned my mother immediately after the reading and told her what you had said. My mother went to a specialist the next week and your diagnosis was correct. My mother is minus her left kidney now but has recovered beautifully. Thank you for saving my mother's life.

—Lucy Anderson-Pollack

Dear Annette:

My friend, Mike Sims, who went down with me to see you, did not fare well. He passed away two weeks ago, following a long bout of illness.

Shortly before he died he said repeatedly that everything you told him had come to pass. His bladder, liver, gallbladder, and just about everything else went to pot all at once just like you saw in the reading. You helped him be ready for his ascent into the light.

—Sylvia Bennett

Annette was a high-energy, sparkling, little hazel-eyed girl, as talented as Shirley Temple and twice as cute. She was on fire to be a singer and actress and, as it turned out, she had bucketsful of talent to go with her ambition.

When she was nine, her parents applied for her to enter the prestigious Elizabeth Halloway School of Drama on Sutter Street in San Francisco, where her talents could be developed. She went there determined to work hard and someday be a star.

That same year her father bought Taraval Hardware on Taraval Street in the Sunset District of San Francisco, a working-class neighborhood west of downtown. The war was over and scrap iron was no longer in high demand, but the do-it-yourself craze was underway, and every do-it-yourselfer had to have tools and hardware. Business was booming.

For her tenth birthday, on December 8, 1947, her parents gave a party for Annette, a combination birthday and going-away party. They were moving to their new neighborhood the next day.

Annette recalls that as the party was winding down, she stepped out onto the front porch. She remembers feeling sad to be leaving her friends on Kissling Street. At first, it seemed like an ordinary evening. The sun was going down. But when she looked at the horizon she saw a strange sight in the reddish, hazy sky. She could see a string of figures appearing, and they kept multiplying. She wondered if they were people. Yes! There were rows of them, hundreds of them, thousands…

What is this? Who are they? she wondered. And then in her head she heard the booming baritone voice of Cama:

These are the people you are going to help in your lifetime.

"What do you mean?" she shouted out loud.

You will help them and make many thousands of people happy, Annette, in your life on earth. Do not be afraid, for they will come to you for help and guidance and you will give it to them.

She felt confused. What did this mean? She had no idea how she could help all those people. Was she to be famous? A doctor? What did she have to learn? Did this mean she couldn't be a celebrated singer or actress? Guide people? How could she guide people?

Cama said nothing more.

No, she thought, she wasn't going to do it. She was going to be a singer and an actress and that was that. She was not going to guide anyone.

Annette, Singer and Actress

In her new home on 31st Avenue, Annette had a new best friend—a golden retriever named Rocheanne. And Annette attended a new school, St. Gabriella's, which she liked. She made many new friends there quickly.

After school she continued her studies to be a performer, and she did well. She was ignoring her psychic visions and blocked them out as best she could; they only got in the way.

By the age of thirteen, Annette had a starring role in the play *Corliss Archer*. Barbara Eden, who would later star in "I Dream of Jeannie" on TV, played Annette's older sister. The theater company toured all the large military bases in California and was a huge hit. Annette was loving it.

By fourteen Annette was doing Gilbert and Sullivan operettas and was picked for the lead in Aaron Copeland's *The Second Hurricane* at

Annette the actress at 13 (center) with Barbara Eden (second from left).

the prestigious San Francisco Conservatory of Music.

Before she was fifteen she was appearing weekly on the Del Courtney Show on local television. People began recognizing her on the street. She was becoming a star; her dream was coming true. She worked with her voice coaches and acting coaches, practiced her singing, played the piano, and everyone predicted she'd be a star.

In 1953, when Annette was sixteen, musical impresario Edwin Lester heard her sing and loved her voice. He came back a year later to hear her again, and shortly afterwards he flew her down to Los Angeles to try out for the role of Milly in the movie *Seven Brides for Seven Brothers*. The directors liked her, but alas, she was still a minor and the studio had just closed their school and could not take a minor for the role without hiring tutors, which the studio was not willing to do. They gave the role instead to Jane Powell, who had a fine operatic voice, and was twenty-four at the time. A tad old for the part, but that's what makeup is for.

By the time she was seventeen, Annette was singing with the Sacramento Music Circus during the summer. Then, after she graduated from Abraham Lincoln High School in San Francisco, she was hired by the San Francisco Civic Light Opera Company and the Los Angeles Civic Light Opera Company, where she sang in the chorus and understudied the parts of Laurey in *Oklahoma* and Mary Martin's Annie in *Annie Get Your Gun*. That production appeared on CBS nationally.

Meanwhile Annette's family moved to Stockton, located in California's hot, dusty, agricultural Central Valley, where her father was supposed to open a new hardware store in a shopping mall near a new housing development. However, the development never happened, and Annette's father was forced back into the junk business.

Annette attended the University of the Pacific in Stockton, but her heart wasn't in it. She wasn't a scholar—she desperately wanted a career in show biz.

Then, one evening while attending a cast party in San Francisco, celebrating the success of the *Oklahoma* production, she had a sudden, inexplicable urge to see a newspaper. She had learned by now that whenever she had such an urge, she should give in to it.

She found a copy of the *San Francisco Chronicle* and started scanning it, not knowing what it was she was looking for—until she spotted an announcement that that very day there were going to be auditions held for the lead in the new comic opera, *The Duchess of Washoe*. Shazam! Her intuition had shown her the way once again. She left the party and took a bus downtown to the audition at the Encore Theater near Union Square.

Her life would never be the same.

Annette in Love

On her way into the theater she heard Cama's voice: *You are about to meet the man you are going to marry.*

Like hell she was, she thought.

She had no intention of marrying, now or ever. She was going to be a star, come hell or high water!

The production of *The Duchess of Washoe* was being directed by the composer, Emil Martin. His son, Dick, was there, on leave from his engineering studies at Stanford.

Annette realized immediately this must be the man Cama had predicted she was going to marry.

He was solidly built on a six-foot-two-inch frame and had clear, blue eyes, a long, straight nose, and an easy smile. All the other girls there to audition, Annette remembers, were all over him. But not her. She wanted nothing to do with him. She did her best to not even look at him. While she was strongly attracted to him, she was determined that Cama's prediction would not come to pass.

She was determined to be a performer and no romantic involvement was going to get in the way. She had seen so many of her colleagues make this disastrous mistake, get sidetracked, lose their focus, and have promising careers go up in smoke. It was not going to happen to her.

Annette got the part of the lead in *The Duchess of Washoe*. She worked hard and the show had a very successful, three-month run. She got to know Dick during that time. He was, she found, not only handsome, but charming, outgoing, friendly, obviously smart, and he had a great sense of humor as well. He had a way of winning people over to his point of view. He was a natural salesman and extremely creative, a problem solver. Everyone liked him. Her infatuation grew, but she kept fighting it. What made it worse, he had a wonderful tenor voice, a well-trained instrument, smooth as honey. When she heard him sing, she remembers, her insides turned to mush.

Annette, 19 years old.

At the end of the run there was the inevitable cast party. Everyone was sad and happy, as usual, and there was a lot of self-congratulation and hugging and tears and laughter. Dick had a car and offered to drive some people home—Annette included.

Annette sat by Dick and they chatted as he drove. Soon he had dropped off everyone and it was only the two of them left—and they were heading in the opposite direction from where she lived.

"I was thinking it might be good if we spent some time together alone—get to know each other better," he said.

Part of her wanted to know him better, sure, but the other part, the good-sense part, didn't. Alarm bells were going off in her dizzy head.

"What do you say?" he said, flashing his warm, easy smile. "Shall we go for a drive?"

"Well, okay…just for a little while," she heard herself say.

Dick drove them out Geary Boulevard to the beach. There was a great orange moon glowing brightly over the vast, gray ocean, she remembers.

As she told me this, Annette seemed to get wispy. Her voice trailed off as she remembered that moon, that beach, that ocean. I asked her what happened.

"He kissed me," she said with a twinkle in her eye. "And it was all over."

Annette and Dick dated over the next two years while she continued her career and he finished his studies at Stanford. Of course she told him about the Gift and promised never to look at him psychically. He found her psychic powers intriguing from the first, and he became a firm believer that she, indeed, had the Gift of the White Light.

Dick had been raised in the teachings of Vedanta, an ancient religion from India that teaches that one can realize God in whatever aspect one wishes, and can realize Him directly and vividly in this life, in this world. Dick's parents also believed in spiritualism, and they even had seances in their home while Dick was growing up. Annette seemed completely normal to the Martin family.

During the two years they dated, Annette discovered Dick had a dark side. Like most creative people, he would sometimes brood, withdrawing not only from her, but from the world. At these times he would be sullen and ill-tempered, almost as if he had a dual personality. But she was desperately in love. When he proposed, she said yes without a second's hesitation.

Annette Meets a Renowned Yogi and Receives a Message

While Dick was finishing his senior year at Stanford University, Annette got a part-time job at the Sherman Clay music store in Sacramento, selling sheet music. She enrolled at Sacramento State College to study drama and voice and landed the role of Tuptim in a student production of *The King and I*. All thoughts of being a psychic were, she thought, behind her. She pushed her psychic visions out of her head as soon as they appeared. She was going to be Mrs. Richard Martin and a singer and actress, and that was that.

The following May she received a telegram from Edwin Lester at the Los Angeles Civic Light Opera Association. He was the impresario who had arranged for her audition at Universal Studios for *Seven Brides for Seven Brothers* when she was sixteen. Now he asked her if she'd come and understudy Laurey in a performance of *Oklahoma* in Los Angeles and sing in the chorus. It promised to be at least a three-month run.

She said yes and started packing. She quit school and her job, and within a few days she was off to Los Angeles.

When she arrived she was delighted to find she knew one of the members of the cast, Bob Piper, having worked with him before. He was a great dancer, and he had performed in almost every Hollywood musical for the previous fifteen years. He was then in his forties with curly hair and big blue eyes and was full of life.

Bob had an abiding interest in all things metaphysical. During rehearsal breaks, he and Annette had a lot to talk about: theater, past lives, reincarnation, and so on. Both of them had done a lot of meditating and were interested in improving their technique.

The cast didn't rehearse on Sundays. One Sunday Bob asked Annette if she'd like to visit the Paramahansa Yogananda meditation center, about five miles from downtown Los Angeles. Sure, she said.

Paramahansa Yogananda, the founder, was a yogi from India who started the center to promote the Self-Realization Fellowship in 1920. His goal was to spread the teachings of Kriya Yoga, a sacred spiritual practice begun millennia ago in India.

The gardens of the center were gorgeous, with weeping willows bending over a beautiful, man-made lake complete with swans. The center was situated high on a hill called by locals "Mount Washington"—actually, a small hill just high enough to offer a stunning panoramic view of the city.

Annette remembers feeling joy and peace at that place. During the ensuing weeks Annette and Bob attended several services there. These services were replete with gongs and chants and incense, glorious sing-ing, and wonderful, joyful dancing. Annette remembers going into sev-eral very deep trances at these services. She loved going there.

Then one Sunday Bob said he had some good news for her—he had spoken to someone very important at the Self-Realization center who wanted to meet her. He would not say who this person was. He acted very secretive, and there was a twinkle in his eye.

The center itself was in the middle of the grounds—a large, three-story, sprawling, white building with a red roof. They went inside. The furniture was sparse, but made of beautifully carved teak. The building reflected the quiet, serene feel of a truly holy place.

Instead of going into the main hall as they usually did, Bob led Annette down a hallway into a large room with floor-to-ceiling win-dows that looked out on the lake and the swans. Sweet incense perfumed the room. On the walls were paintings of deities and spiritual masters. At the end of the room was a raised platform with a woman in the yellow saffron robes of a yogi seated on red, overstuffed pillows. She had soft, brown skin and long, shimmering black hair that cascaded over her shoul-ders. Behind her was an enormous oil painting of the center's founder, Yogananda, standing in a garden wearing his brilliant saffron robes, a look of serenity on his face.

As she approached, Annette could see the woman's eyes were closed; she was in deep meditation, looking radiantly beautiful. Peace and seren-ity emanated from her. Her aura was pure white, the whitest Annette had ever seen.

Bob guided Annette to sit on a red-and-yellow pillow and he whispered for her to wait for the woman to speak. Then he left the room. Annette sat and waited, feeling excited and tense. The woman did not move. She hardly breathed. Annette had no idea why this woman wanted to speak to her and couldn't imagine what she'd have to say.

A quarter of an hour went by before the woman finally opened her large, serene, brown eyes, —eyes that looked steadily straight ahead, not at Annette. After a moment, the woman said in halting English:

"My child, you must go out into the world, not stay cloistered. Go out into the world and teach them…teach them of the Light. For the good of their minds and bodies and souls. You will help many with your love and the Gift of the Light. You will help them to see what they themselves do not see."

And with that, she closed her eyes and said no more, returning to a deep trance state, almost not breathing.

Annette sat there trembling and speechless, stunned. This is what Cama had said to her when she was eleven!

Bob appeared a few moments later and they went outside. They sat by the lake. Annette was still trembling; tears ran down her cheeks. Bob explained that this lady was Sri Daya Mata, Yogananda's disciple, personally trained by him. She was one of but a few women in history to lead a worldwide religious movement. He added that before she spoke to Annette, she had been in Samahdi, the deepest state of meditation possible.

Annette knew that Samahdi was a state in which the individual mind, freed from time and from all material limits, experienced total bliss and enlightenment. She had never reached that state herself.

She told Bob that what the woman said was almost word-for-word what her spirit guide had told her when she was a child.

"You see, Annette, you indeed are supposed to do this work." He stared at her, his mouth open, as if seeing something truly amazing. "At this moment the light around you is breathtaking."

"But I want to be a singer and an actress, like Jane Powell," Annette said. "How can I teach all these people all these things?"

He didn't know, he said, but he was sure she would be shown the way.

She didn't want this Gift of the White Light; she only wanted to sing and to act. Yet it was difficult to go against Cama and Sri Daya Mata. Perhaps, as Bob said, she'd be shown the way.

Annette remembers they sat for a long time by that lake, feeling the great, loving energy that surrounds the center and the beautiful grounds.

Annette Becomes Mrs. Martin

Dick and Annette eloped to Reno on November 3, 1959.

Soon, Dick got a job with General Electric, marketing capacitors, and Annette and Dick moved to Glens Falls, New York. Once settled in, Annette sang at Glens Falls Operatic Theater and at the Lake George

Light Opera Company. She was acting and singing in outrageous melo-dramas and vaudeville. Their first child, Craig, was born August 23, 1960, in Glens Falls. Annette remembers the few years they spent there as being happy ones.

Then Dick got another promotion and they moved to Gainesville, Florida, where Scott, their second son, was born on June 2, 1963. Annette hated Florida: the snakes, the heat, the dampness; and worse, the climate agitated Craig's allergies, which quickly turned into asthma. Annette re-calls they almost lost him three times and had to rush him to the emer-gency room in the middle of the night.

But then, luckily, within a year and a half, Dick was promoted again, and the family moved to Syracuse, New York.

Here they bought a split-level home in suburban Fayetteville and Annette became involved with the Syracuse Opera Company, perform-ing *Once Upon a Mattress*. Promoters were about to star her in a new, local TV show when, oops, Dick, the hotshot salesman, landed a great new job with Fairchild Semiconductors in northern California's Silicon Valley, near where both Annette and Dick had grown up and where they both had family and friends.

So, Annette and Dick sold the house, said good-bye to the snowy, cold winters and muggy, hot summers of upstate New York, and off they went to sunny California, happy as oranges ripening in the sun.

There they built a new home in suburban Saratoga and settled in for what Annette hoped would be a good, long stay. She involved herself in decorating the house, gardening, coffee klatches with the neighbors, raising the boys, entertaining, and trying hard not to be psychic.

Both Dick and Annette joined the West Bay Opera Company in Palo Alto, directed by the renowned conductor Henry Holt. Annette was in paradise. She was living near her family and friends, had a beautiful new home, two great kids, a successful husband with a soaring career, and she was a member of a wonderful musical company. She landed a lot of good supporting roles and lead roles in *Pagliacci* and *Il Campanello*.

Things were going great.

Then one Fourth of July, after what Annette recalls as a wonderful day with the family—Craig was then almost nine and Scott was six—Dick asked her to come sit with him on the couch. She snuggled up next to him. They'd been to a picnic with family and friends, had watched the fireworks, and were tired. It had been a good day, a fun day. She remembers Dick kicked up his feet; he lit a Cuban cigar, took a few puffs, and whispered a question in her ear: How'd she like to live in Hong Kong? It meant another promotion: He would be head of Fairchild Semiconductors' marketing operation in Asia.

Annette could see in his eyes that he was dying to go. It meant leaving a lot of family and friends, uprooting the kids, but hey…it sounded like an adventure. Annette knew that when you're a corporate wife, you've always got to be ready to call the movers. She was ready.

They sold their house and, six weeks later, boarded a plane for Hong Kong. It was August 1969.

Dick became seriously ill on the plane. He had an extremely high fever and looked yellow as a canary. Annette forgot her determination to turn off her powers and scanned him psychically. He would recover.

As she helped Dick off the 747, she heard Cama's voice again. It said: *Now is the time.*

Time for what? She had no idea. Later, though, she would understand that this message marked the beginning of her life as a professional psychic.

But first, there was the trouble settling in.

Hong Kong was, at the time of Annette and her family's arrival, a colony of Great Britain. Hong Kong consisted of a harbor, a small slice of the mainland, and several islands: a British boil on the backside of Communist China. Though encompassing an area of only 422 square miles, Hong Kong was teeming with people—nearly six million of them—most of them pajama-clad Chinese peasants.

Hong Kong was a world banking, manufacturing, and trading center, its harbor crammed with ships of perhaps a hundred nations—as well as thousands of Chinese junks and sampans, their white anchor lights twinkling like stars in the dark of night. These small coastal boats that lined the shores and docks provided a means of transportation and a living to fishermen and smugglers, as well as a home to perhaps two million people.

Hong Kong was a beehive of commercial activity.

As soon as Annette and her family checked into their hotel, Annette called a doctor for Dick, who was getting more miserable by the minute. The doctor looked him over, poked and prodded, called for an ambulance, and Dick was whisked off to a hospital on top of a high hill in the center of Hong Kong Island. It was quickly determined that Dick had a case of hepatitis, and he would need to be hospitalized for a month.

Annette's life quickly became a fury of activity. Between visiting her poor, sick husband in the hospital, learning to drive on the left side of the road, setting up their apartment, hiring some domestic help, and getting the boys ready for school, Annette was feeling like she was caught up in a typhoon.

Chapter Five

Annette Gets into the Psychic Biz

In the August issue (of FATE Magazine), I focused my column on Annette Martin, a psychic practitioner here in the Bay Area. The intro to the article mentioned a woman whom Annette kept insisting should see a doctor. Recently, Annette got a follow-up call about this woman, who we'll call Sandy, and forwarded the information to me. Annette had perceived a problem with Sandy's heart…Sandy's doctors ended up putting in a pacemaker. Without it, her future was very likely nonexistent. Today, Sandy is doing well and no longer suffers from blackouts.
—Loyd Auerbach

You were right, Annette; I have walking pneumonia…went to doctor Monday…he prescribed massive dose of antibiotics…I am on the mend.
—Patti Wilson

Despite being busy with her duties as a corporate wife and mother, Annette soon found herself swamped with customers for her psychic services.

People she didn't know were calling her at all hours of the day and night desperate for her to do psychic readings. It was puzzling: She had no idea how anyone knew she was psychic. She certainly hadn't told anyone. She didn't even know anyone, except for a few of Dick's corporate acquaintances, and she hadn't told any of them. She found she had a hard time turning anyone down who needed her help, so she almost always said yes, no matter how busy she was.

A month or so after Dick came home from the hospital, he insisted she do something to stop the flood of phone calls they were getting. The psychic business was, he said, severely disturbing their domestic tranquility.

Annette had a plan: She'd charge for readings. That would certainly cut down the traffic. When she received her next request, she quoted what she thought was a pretty stiff price. Made no difference. Somehow the word had gotten around that she was an extraordinary psychic, and people were willing to pay.

Doing these readings, Annette remembers now, was at first slow. Since she had little experience at it, she was honing her technique daily. She would sit in her meditation position, upright in a chair, and close her eyes and put her hands on her lap, palms up. She would then take in three deep breaths through her nostrils and exhale through her mouth, while visualizing the White Light. She'd see it shining on her from above, entering her body through the top of her head. She'd wait and, after a moment, a feeling or words would come to her.

Her spirit guide, Cama, she says, once told her that both prayer and meditation were forms of communicating with God and they are very good things to do. She had always done a lot of meditating and a lot of praying, and she found herself doing even more now.

She made a new friend: Faye, the wife of one of Dick's marketing executives. Faye asked Annette if she'd like to join a yoga class she was taking to help her handle all the stress she was under. Faye was fascinated by Annette's psychic adventures. She suggested that maybe Annette could do some readings at her house for some of her friends. Annette agreed and within a few days she had set up several sessions.

Recalling those early medical readings, Annette said, "Sometimes it would seem like an eternity before a picture, words, or a feeling would emerge."

She said the average time was about two minutes, which was certainly a long time, just sitting there hoping and praying that you will see something for the person sitting across from you.

In the beginning she worried that she wouldn't see anything at all and she worried a lot about what she would tell the client if there was nothing there. It made her feel very uneasy. It took a while to build her confidence.

When it had come to singing or acting and performing in front of a crowd, it was different, as she knew what she was going to sing or say and where she was to move on the stage. It had been rehearsed and rehearsed—but with this, she was winging it.

She experimented with "automatic writing." In a trance, she'd make two or three circles and a few lines and then words would appear "as if by magic." She says she was absolutely in an altered state and would never remember afterwards what she had written.

She was only vaguely aware then that what she was doing was trance-channeling from the spirit world. The clients would ask questions about their loved ones who had passed over and the spirits would answer quite clearly. They'd speak about love and forgiveness and, always, the spirits were reassuring that they were alive even though they were dead, and that they were happy and content in the spirit world.

Trance-channeling was a skill Annette would need later when working with detectives. Of course she had no idea at the time what she'd be doing with it. Here, in Hong Kong, she was in training, gaining confidence, honing her techniques. She found that the more she worked at it, the better she got, the faster the images and voices would come, and the easier it became to interpret the images. She was indeed becoming a pro.

Annette on the Loose

When she wasn't seeing clients, Annette roamed the streets and alleys of Hong Kong, visiting antique shops and furniture stores. The place was one vast market, selling exotic teas and spices, handmade hardwood furniture, beautiful silks, jewelry, and all kinds of artworks and bric-a-brac to the tourists that packed the streets, rubbing elbows with the coolies in their pointed, brimmed hats, many pulling rickshaws. Annette remembers going down narrow, dark alleys, passing by the open doors of opium dens and seeing the customers on cots with canopies over them. She vividly recalls smelling the sweet scent of the opium.

Annette found Hong Kong energizing. The Chinese people seemed to have an affinity for her, and she for them. She found them friendly and kind; she was in love with the place.

She began collecting antique, handmade tapestries and Mandarin sleeves and Mandarin squares; these were civil and military emblems showing various kinds of birds, which were symbols of officialdom in Imperial China. Annette now believes she has one of the largest private collections of these artifacts in the world. In fact, years later she would host a showing of her collection at the Hilton Hotel near Chinatown in San Francisco that would draw 60,000 people.

Before going to Hong Kong, Annette had no idea such things even existed, but once she saw them she immediately became a collector. Finding new pieces of quality was difficult because there were many frauds and imitations, but she soon discovered that not only was the White Light guiding her in the selection of the pieces, it was leading her down the labyrinth of streets and alleys in the old section where the pieces she needed for her collection were to be found. Time and time again she would be led to the right shop on the right day where she'd find just the right piece.

Annette started singing with both the Hong Kong Musical Theater and the Hong Kong Symphony. At home there was a parade of guests— friends and relatives from the states—and there were corporate get-togethers, and she seemed to be constantly running the kids to baseball practice and school outings. Annette was one busy lady, but happy. She was having a great time in an exotic wonderland.

A Strange Visitor

On October 5, 1969, at a little after ten in the evening, a strange visitor appeared. The kids were in bed, Dick was out at a business dinner with executives from Japan Airlines, and the house was quiet. Annette had gone to bed. She'd read for a while and was just reaching to turn off the light when she sensed some movement.

She felt a chill. Someone—or something—was at the foot of her bed! She felt a momentous event was about to happen, but she didn't have a clue as to what it might be. Her heart beat fast.

Then she saw a mist begin to form—as it had when she was eleven and Cama had appeared to her. Since the first few times, Cama had not come with the mist; he just appeared to Annette instantly.

So what could this be? The mist took the shape of a man.

She was frightened and strangely disoriented; she felt an intense, eerie chill. She pulled the covers up over her head. "No!" she cried. "I don't want to see you!"

She remembered how terrified her cousin Candy had been when she saw creepy apparitions and wanted no part of them.

There was no sound. Nothing at all. Nothing touched her. All she could hear was the sound of her own breathing. After a few moments she took a peek.

The man stood at the foot of the bed, smiling at her. He wore a suit and tie and had a pleasant, serene face. She squinted. She knew him! He was Henry Holt, founder and conductor of the West Bay Opera Company for whom she had sung for Palo Alto, California! He had been a wonderful friend to her and she loved him as she would a kind grandfather. He had also coached her lovingly and skillfully for the auditions to the Merola training program with the San Francisco Opera.

"Mr. Holt! Henry! What are you doing here? Welcome to Hong Kong!" She started to slide out of bed to greet him, but he held up his hand.

"Annette, I am sorry if I startled you," he whispered in his gentle, Bavarian accent. "I have come to say good-bye. I will miss you. Take good care of yourself." He faded away and all that was left was a mist that slowly dissipated.

Annette was too astonished to speak.

Annette was still sitting on the edge of the bed, tears running down her face, when Dick arrived home some time later.

"You look like you've seen a ghost," he said. "You all right?" He sat beside her and put his arm around her to stop her shivering.

She had been sitting there trying to make sense of what she had seen. She asked him if he remembered the going-away party the West Bay Opera Company had thrown for them when they'd gone to Hong Kong. He said he did. Annette asked if he remembered what Henry Holt had said when they said their good-byes.

"I'm not sure," he said.

"He took hold of my shoulders and said, 'No, Annette, we cannot say good-bye now. I'll see you again, and then we'll say good-bye.'"

Dick nodded. "Yes, he did say that."

They had both thought it strange at the time. They had no idea what he meant.

Annette and Dick called Annette's mother in California to check on Henry to see if he was all right.

Later, when Annette's mother called back, she told them she'd phoned the Holt household and discovered that Henry Holt had died in Palo Alto. It turned out that he had died a few moments before the apparition appeared to Annette in Hong Kong—with the sixteen-hour time difference taken into account.

Annette felt sad and unsettled over this event. She'd lost a dear friend. He had been so kind to her when he was her mentor back in Palo Alto.

Annette recalls now how this event changed her sense of time and space. On the psychic plane, time and space were now blurred together: Hong Kong and California were really not far apart; in fact, they were really the same place, she thought.

Another Apparition

Annette and Dick went to dinner at the home of some friends, Joyce and Don, whom they had met at the American Club. Joyce and Don had a flat in the same apartment complex as Annette and Dick. Don was yet another engineer. He was a tall, thin man, with lots of curly brown hair; his demeanor was stiff and serious and he was very smart.

Joyce was plump and thirty-ish, an Italian American. She had chestnut-brown hair and was outgoing and effusive, but she was often depressed. She was a good amateur artist in oils and acrylics, producing mostly modern abstracts. Annette remembers her as a warm, friendly person, often gloomy, but a good friend.

The plan was to have drinks and dinner at Joyce and Dick's and Annette would do a psychic reading for Joyce, who had a keen interest in the paranormal. Don was tolerant, but skeptical about things metaphysical.

It was summer and blistering hot; the humidity was nearly 100 percent. Annette wore a frilly, white blouse. The blouse, stylish in those days, had puffy sleeves that stuck up perhaps six inches.

The flat, thankfully, was air-conditioned. The dinner was American style: steak, vegetables, and potatoes, topped off by a scrumptious chocolate cake. They were seated at a long, narrow, antique oak table that Joyce and Don had bought in Europe the year before. Dick and Don were seated at the ends, Annette and Joyce on the sides.

Joyce had just brought the cake to the table and was starting to cut it when Annette felt a chill coming on. She sensed an energy field around her.

"What's happening?" she asked, looking around.

Everyone shrugged. They didn't see anything. Everyone was quiet.

Annette began to feel a gentle pressure on her left shoulder. Frightened, she fought back tears. "What is it?" she whispered. "What's going on?" The pressure was getting stronger.

"Look!" Joyce cried, eyes wide, pointing to Annette's shoulder. Her blouse, the frilly part that stuck up, was flattened as if someone were pushing down on it.

Dick was on his feet. "I see it too!" he exclaimed.

Don kept shaking his head. "I don't believe what I'm seeing."

A mist was forming all around Annette's body. She went rigid with fear, her heart pounding. It felt like a hand pressing hard on her shoulder—yet no one was there!

Then Annette heard a voice in her head:

I am Edgar Cayce. They call me 'the sleeping prophet." Stay calm, Annette—I will not harm you. I have come to assist you with your health readings.

Annette repeated the words as he said them, tears streaming down her face. Everyone was transfixed.

Annette had never heard of Edgar Cayce, but Joyce had, and she was nearly overcome to hear the name of the eminent, long-departed psychic.

The apparition said: *You will be able to see me so that you know that I am present.*

Annette said she was afraid, and asked if she had to see him.

It will be all right, he said, and Annette repeated it.

Joyce kept saying that she couldn't see anything but a mist.

Then, out of the mist, Cayce appeared to Annette: a slight figure of a man in a wrinkled, black suit and a beat-up, black hat that looked to

Annette as if it had been sat on. She was no longer afraid. She described him to the others. Joyce trembled, tears streaming down her face. Dick fell back in his chair with amazement. "Edgar Cayce, imagine."

Then, for the next several minutes, Edgar Cayce did a medical reading for Joyce through Annette, both physical and psychological. Annette repeated it so quickly that Don had trouble writing it down. Joyce had fibroids and would need a hysterectomy; she had a hormone imbalance and was diabetic; she was manic depressive…he continued on in great detail.

When he finished, he said good-bye and vanished into the mist, which then dissipated. Annette collapsed into her chair, exhausted yet exhilarated. "He's gone," she said.

Joyce was hysterical, crying and laughing, saying she knew that some of what he said was true, but some she'd have to check with her doctor. Annette suggested she do so as soon as possible.

A few days later Annette heard from Joyce. She said she had been feeling ill for some time, but was too afraid to go to a doctor. She said she'd been confused and was harboring suicidal thoughts. But now she'd had a battery of tests and was seeing some specialists and she was getting back into control. She added:

"You and Mr. Cayce saved my life, Annette. My reading was absolutely, totally correct."

Later, Joyce presented Annette with a white pearl ring set in 24-karat gold as a thank-you. Annette wears the ring to this day.

Afterwards, Annette realized that Edgar Cayce had been helping her for some time, whispering to her in her mind during her readings. She felt honored.

Edgar Cayce

Edgar Cayce was perhaps the most famous American psychic who ever lived. There have been over 300 books written about him, and thousands of articles. He was born near Hopkinsville, Kentucky, in 1877, the son of a farmer. As in Annette's case, he had relatives with psychic powers. His grandfather was said to be able to make brooms dance—and was a "water witch" with a legendary ability to find water.

As a young man, Edgar Cayce had wanted to be a preacher, but he mysteriously lost his voice at age twenty-one and could only speak in a whisper, so preaching was out. Instead, he made his living as a photographer and did odd jobs.

In an effort to effect a cure for his speech impediment, he sought the services of Al Layne, a local hypnotist. During the session it was discovered that Cayce could speak normally while in a trance, and could even diagnose his own problem: a lack of blood circulation in the area of the voice box. The hypnotist was amazed when Cayce managed to give himself a posthypnotic suggestion that cured the problem.

It was soon discovered that Cayce could accurately diagnose other people's illnesses as well, and he could give detailed instructions for how to cure them. Cayce barely had a sixth-grade education, yet he often diagnosed rare diseases he couldn't possibly have known about, and he suggested obscure medicines, even though he had absolutely no knowledge of them while he was awake. His accuracy as a diagnostician was amazing, and often the cures he recommended were extremely effective treatments. Amazingly, he could diagnose and treat sick people at a distance by teleporting himself into their presence.

His fame spread. He was both revered and reviled, hailed as a prophet by some, and denounced as a fraud, a liar, a cheat, and a blasphemer by others.

He had others keep a detailed transcript of everything he said while in a trance, and these transcripts have been preserved. They number over 14,000!

While in a waking state, Cayce could not remember anything he said during a trance, which is why he was called "the sleeping prophet." A devoted, fundamentalist Christian, he read the Bible avidly every day. As a boy he could learn the contents of schoolbooks without ever reading them by simply sleeping on them. Hey, now there's a useful skill for a schoolboy!

At first, he only did medical readings and advised people on health issues. But then in the late 1920s he started reading people's past lives. Cayce was deeply troubled by these revelations, since reincarnation did not sit well with his deeply-held fundamentalist Christian beliefs. Many of his Christian supporters abandoned him over this issue. Despite his misgivings, he continued doing past lives readings right up to his death.

He also began to make predictions about future events and to reveal things about the past he had no way of knowing. As an example, archeologists had long dated the Sphinx in Egypt at about 4,500 years. Edgar Cayce was widely ridiculed when he said that it was 10,500 years old, older than the Egyptian civilization itself!

Only recently has science caught up with Mr. Cayce. In the early 1990s, Egyptologist John Anthony West and Boston University geology professor Robert M. Schoch, through a study of erosion patterns, demonstrated conclusively that the Sphinx is at least 9,000 years old. Nobody's laughing at Mr. Cayce's revelation any more.

Many other predictions Edgar Cayce made have come to pass: two world wars, the assassination of a president, and a war (possibly a world war) in the area of the Persian Gulf, Syria, Libya, and Egypt.

While it's true that other of his predictions have not as yet come true—China has not turned Christian and California has not been destroyed by an earthquake—he still had an impressive list of successes, and some of the events he predicted may yet come to pass.

At the end of his life, Edgar Cayce wrote:

> *The life of a person endowed with such powers is not easy. For more than forty years now I have been giving readings to those who came seeking help. Thirty-five years ago the jeers, scorn, and laughter were even louder than today. I have faced the laughter of ignorant crowds, the withering scorn of tabloid headlines, and the cold smirk of self-satisfied intellectuals. But I have also known the wordless happiness of little children who have been helped, the gratitude of fathers and mothers and friends...*

From that day in Joyce and Don's dining room in Hong Kong where Edgar Cayce first appeared to Annette, he has been mystically, lovingly, helpfully at her side every time she's done a reading, Annette says. Sometimes he gives her advice; sometimes he merely stands by. She sees him just as she did when she first saw him over thirty years ago: a shy, sweet, giving person—a slightly built little man in a wrinkled black suit and a beat-up hat.

Annette's Psychic Biz Booms

Once word of Edgar Cayce's appearance spread around the tiny American ex-patriot community in Hong Kong, Annette was deluged with requests for readings. Annette was still torn between trying to keep up with her domestic responsibilities, her singing career, building her collection of Mandarin sleeves, and being a full-time psychic.

She didn't truly think of herself as a professional psychic; it was something she just happened to be good at and would do it because people needed her. She still had hopes of being an opera star and had a heavy rehearsal and performance schedule with the Hong Kong Singers.

But she did squeeze in medical and general life readings whenever she could. At that time she did not routinely record her sessions, as she would do later, but she did record a few of them at the request of the person she was doing the reading for, and one lone recording has survived out of the several hundred she did while living in Hong Kong. This recording is presented here as an example of a typical session.

The client was "Beverly G.," the wife of an American business executive in Hong Kong. This session took place in the living room of Annette's flat. Only Annette and the client were present.

> ANNETTE: I see a picture of you standing on some big rocks, looking down at the ocean. You really enjoy that because I see you becoming very calm.
>
> BEVERLY G.: I've stood on a lot of rocks at the ocean in my life. That's so true; it's my therapy!
>
> ANNETTE: My ears suddenly plugged up. Do both of your ears plug up when you go out to the ocean? I hear the wind whistling through them. Do you know that you are disturbed by atmospheric changes?
>
> BEVERLY G.: Yes, I do and I am disturbed by them!
>
> ANNETTE: How interesting, because that is exactly what Mr. Edgar Cayce is saying to me. There is a little canal in the ear and it pulsates when there is an atmospheric change and closes up, which makes them feel plugged up. You can still hear, but they're plugged up. Your body is super-sensitive to atmospheric changes! Okay, Mr. Edgar Cayce says that as you slow down your breathing and become very calm it will lower your bodily temperature and that will change your inside metabolic rate, which will affect everything and will open the ears and put them back

into a normal state. Do you get pressure across here? [*Annette points to her forehead*]

BEVERLY G.: Yes, I do!

ANNETTE: That has to do with the atmosphere also. Pressure goes up. The same thing is lowering the body temperature…I am going to move further down the body. The throat tightens up. When you get upset, you get very, very tight. You can hardly talk.

BEVERLY G.: Yes, that's so true!

ANNETTE: The voice gets very funny. That's nerves causing that. If you could just isolate this and concentrate when this happens to you and start deep breathing and projecting to the throat that it must relax, you're not going to get upset and you're not going to tighten up here. Keep talking to it and telling it to relax. It's difficult when you are angry but if you can try and do it you can teach yourself and pretty soon all you will have to do is send the thoughts down there, "When I am angry my throat will not tighten up!" You can program yourself…Do you sing? I hear you singing. Do you sing folk songs?

BEVERLY G.: Yes, yes, I do folk songs! You're amazing, Annette!

ANNETTE: That's another reason why you shouldn't tighten up there. Doesn't help. That will promote nodes on the vocal cords. By tightening up, you have to have it all be very loose. Oh, I feel that the glands hurt, right here. [*Annette points to her neck*]

BEVERLY G.: Yes, I've had some problems there!

ANNETTE: Boy, you sure have. Mr. Edgar Cayce recommends that every morning you take a huge cup of warm water with lemon and honey. That will help to keep the glands clean, as they are very swollen. And whatever you do, don't sing when the glands are swollen…All right, I am going to move further down the body. Oh, I am seeing supersensitive breasts.

BEVERLY G.: Yes!

ANNETTE: Even if someone comes near you, you go crazy! They also look lopsided, like one is lower than the other.

BEVERLY G.: Yes, they are, and I can't stand anyone hugging me, or the doctor examining me, as they hurt so much.

ANNETTE: I am seeing a glandular problem; the glands are very sensitive, extremely.

BEVERLY G.: Yes, definitely! Is there something that I can do?

ANNETTE: It's out of balance and I see the doctor giving you shots for the glands. Something for the glands. I see a shot going into the hips. [*pause*] I am seeing something that is in a horseshoe effect. They're standing out in an x-ray form; they are white and they're standing out. I keep seeing… They look like tubes—yes, that's it—tubes.

BEVERLY G.: Yes, that's very true!

ANNETTE: I am seeing an operation. Tubal ligation! Tubal ligation!

BEVERLY G.: Yes, that's it! I had that operation several months ago.

ANNETTE: I am very cold—your temperature went way down. Trauma, this caused trauma. The glands are all funny, like they're shocked. And they haven't been right since. They all went screwy.

BEVERLY G.: Right!

ANNETTE: Mr. Edgar Cayce is saying that they didn't give you anything to put you back normally. They haven't been giving you anything to regulate the hormones and the glands! You're just woozing and woozing.

BEVERLY G.: That's absolutely right!

ANNETTE: I feel seasick. That's what it is. Okay, the doctor is going to give you some shots, a shot in the hip, that will straighten out the hormones and the glands. The glands will calm down in conjunction with the hormones. My lord, it's like being on a ship. Being seasick and the whole thing all the time. Even my knees feel weak.

BEVERLY G.: Annette, that is just what I feel like, all of the time.

The session ended.

Beverly G.'s doctor gave her steroid shots in the hip for several months and she was cured.

Chapter Six

The Writing on the Wall and Ghostly Visits

Dear Annette:

Years ago, when I was six months pregnant I went to you for a reading. You saw a female child with a "sunny" personality and strawberry blond hair. You said that she would have an interest in singing, playing music, dancing, and perhaps acting. You said you saw her loving animals and angels. Physically, you saw her as being very tall. She would have a tendency to have nasal stuffiness and weakness in one ankle (probably the right ankle).

You were right on all accounts! We named our girl Jeanie. Today, Jeanie sings with the San Francisco Girl's Chorus and church choir and has done some solo work at her school. She loves to dance and has taken tap lessons for years; She also plays the piano and says that music is her life! Jeanie is also doing some acting in the school plays and loves that as well. She is five feet eight inches and still growing. Jeanie has had a pony, a horse, and a cow since she was seven-years-old and spends many hours talking to them. Jeanie has had hay fever that causes a stuffiness in her nose and her right ankle is very weak, since birth.

You are really unbelievable!
—Claudia Sinclair

Annette Martin, during my reading saw cysts in my breast but said that they were nonmalignant and would disappear in time. Indeed they did and later a doctor told me the same thing, not to worry.
—Sally J. Johnson

Dear Annette,

Many days have passed where my thoughts have sought you out. I am enclosing a copy of the medical certificate. You told me in the reading that I needed a hysterectomy and to please see my gynecologist as soon as possible. I followed your feelings, even though I had no symptoms of problems and made an appointment. As you can see from the certificate, you were absolutely right. He operated three weeks later.

You're such a beautiful person.

—Holly Clark

One evening in January 1971, Annette and Dick invited two engineers to dine with them. They were visiting Hong Kong from Fairchild's main plant in Sunnyvale, California. While Annette and Dick were greeting their guests in the vestibule, Annette heard Cama's voice in her head, loudly proclaiming that one of the men—the one in the brown sport coat—would soon be living in Annette and Dick's apartment!

Annette says Cama always speaks loudly, as if she were deaf. This time, she remembers, he was really hollering.

Of course she had to ignore him. What would her guests think if they suspected she were having a conversation with voices in her head?

But why had he said this man was going to be living in their apartment? She was shaken. Dick said later that she seemed suddenly pale. He thought she might be ill.

In her head she was answering Cama: *Why would you say he's going to live in our apartment? We're not leaving. We love Hong Kong!*

Cama does not like to be argued with. As they moved into the living room, she could see through the archways into the dining room, where writing suddenly appeared on the wall in foot-and-a-half-high, thick, black letters: THIS IS THE MAN WHO IS SOON GOING TO BE LIVING IN THIS APARTMENT.

Annette swallowed. Thank goodness only she could see the writing.

Dick came over to her and asked her in a whisper if anything was wrong.

She'd have to tell him later.

Wing, their cook, served drinks and hors d'oeuvres. Annette finally had settled down. Cama was never wrong. Oh, well, if they were giving up the apartment she might as well give their guest the royal tour. And, to Dick's amazement, that's what she did.

Later, after the engineers had gone back to their hotel, Dick asked her what had happened. She told him what Cama had told her.

Dick scoffed. "Impossible," he said. "I have a three-year contract. It's just not possible."

A few weeks later Dick came home and announced he'd been offered the position of general manager of the Fairchild plant in Mexico City.

Annette smiled.

"Guess who's taking over my job at the plant—and our apartment here?"

Annette didn't bother to guess. She merely said it was so nice he got to look around the night he came to dinner.

Welcome to Mexico

Always eager for new experiences, Annette looked forward to their time in Mexico City, the ancient capital of the Aztecs. She was excited about encountering a new culture, meeting new people, tasting exotic foods, and getting acquainted with Mexico's rich and colorful history. There were colonial palaces to see, and world-class museums, and plenty of glitzy shopping districts, fine tourist restaurants, splendid parks. At that time, Mexico City, with over twenty million people, was the largest city in the world.

Upon her arrival, Annette was disappointed. She found choking brown air, noise, suffocating crowds, the constant drone and beeping of noisy traffic, and overcrowded slums.

In Hong Kong, the Chinese were friendly and welcoming: She'd been made to feel at home. In Mexico City, the people seemed stand-offish and not very polite; she felt alien and unwelcome. And she soon found she had a problem adapting to some of the deeply entrenched customs.

One of them had to do with customs regarding the police, and the paying of bribes.

After she was there for just a few weeks, Annette was driving a rental car down a main boulevard. She made a left turn where the arrows indicated turning left was permitted, but a cop stopped her to give her a ticket anyway. She spoke no Spanish. The cop spoke no English.

With the use of hand gestures, she pointed out that a left turn was permitted. Bystanders communicated to her mostly by hand signals that what the cop wanted was a small bribe, which, of course, she had already figured out. Annette, as a matter of principle, does not pay bribes in Mexico City or anyplace else. The officer was not going to let this gringa get away without paying her bribe, so he arrested her and attempted to take her to the *calaboose*.

Annette did not agree with this plan.

She screamed and yelled, creating a small riot on the street corner, gathering a large crowd that soon attracted a police supervisor, and his supervisor, and finally the chief of police—who did speak English. She explained her side of it. The chief diplomatically sided with her, much to the crowd's approval. She was released, and she received an apology.

Still, the incident left a bad taste in Annette's mouth.

A few days later she came down with a horrific case of dysentery caused by killer amoebas, even though she had been careful to wash her vegetables and only drink bottled water—even to brush her teeth. She was dreadfully sick and took weeks to recover. Her doctor told her that it was a good thing she'd come in right away, as the particular type of amoebas she had encountered can cause irreparable damage to the kidneys. Afterwards she worried constantly about what she was eating and drinking. She did not like feeling that she had to be always on guard against nasty amoebas and crooked cops. Annette and Mexico had gotten off to a bad start.

The family moved into a spacious, two-story, end-unit, Mexican-style condo on a steep, cobblestone dead-end street in the suburb of Mexico City called Techamachelco. The floors of the condo had wide, blue-and-yellow Spanish tiles in the kitchen and bathrooms, and the stairs leading to the second floor had gleaming, black-enameled, wooden banisters. The place had a rustic feel, which Annette liked. However, the master bedroom hung out over a ravine that she did not like. She did not think much of Mexican workmanship.

Nor did she think much of the mañana attitude when it came to service. "Mañana," as anyone who has had more than a day-and-a-half of high school Spanish knows, means "tomorrow." Visitors to Mexico will argue with this definition; they claim it means "someday." Annette felt the mañana attitude seemed to permeate Mexican culture. For workmen to be late for an appointment—or not show up at all—seemed to be a point of pride.

Annette's family condo was two miles outside of Mexico City, which presented a problem for delivery of services. They had chosen that particular area because of the cleaner air. Craig, Annette's oldest boy, had asthma, and they could never take him downtown for fear the smog might kill him.

Later, when the cold weather set in, Annette decided Craig needed a heater in his room, as there was no central heat in any of the condos. She ordered a heater from Sears. Craig already had a bad cold and was freezing at night because he tossed his blankets off in his sleep. The manager at Sears assured her the man would be out to install it the next day. Mañana. Annette was delighted to find that the man showed up the next day. The trouble was, he merely placed the heater in Craig's room, but did not hook it up.

The man did not speak much English, and Annette was still using tourist Spanish, but she was able to elicit from him the fact that he was not hooking it up now and would be back mañana. As he was walking out the door, Annette says she absolutely and completely and totally lost it. She grabbed a gigantic kitchen knife from the kitchen counter and took off after him, yelling at him in English to come back, while he stumbled down the hill yelling who knows what Spanish obscenities back over his shoulder.

Annette says this is the only time in her life she seriously wanted to hurt someone. Hurt him badly. The neighbors and her maid and her boys were amused to see Annette doing battle. Her boys still remind her of this episode every now and then.

Annette was not getting along well in Mexico, but she was determined to stick it out. After all, if her husband needed to be here for his work, she would support him, and do it cheerfully.

Craig and Scott at first did not get on well in school. The lessons were in Spanish, and they didn't know one word of the language. But after a month or so they started to catch on and soon were pretty much bilingual, to Annette's delight.

So things were looking up.

She soon found she was feeling relieved that she had no reputation here as a psychic and was not, therefore, besieged by clients demanding readings. She could devote her energies to her first love: singing.

Dick's company provided the services of the servienta (maid), Carmalita, who did all the buying at the market, the cooking, and most of the domestic chores, so Annette was free to become a full-time singer.

Not long after their arrival, Annette and Dick were invited to a dinner party given by a competitor, General Electric. At the party she met a world-class opera singer, Franco Iglesias, who subsequently gave Annette singing lessons and coached her on numerous opera roles. She was soon performing the lead role in the Mexico City Light Opera Company's production of *La Boheme*, and later she sang the mother's role in *Amahl and the Night Visitors*, along with her son Scott, who in his first-ever performance played the role of Amahl. Annette remembers Scott memorized the role in nothing flat and sang like he'd been singing for years. He had a natural voice. Annette was a very proud mother.

The following year, Franco Iglesias arranged for Annette to meet Placido Domingo, one of the world's greatest tenors at the time. Annette sang for him, and she remembers vividly how difficult it was to sing with her knees knocking together. But Placido Domingo was gracious and warm and, she was certain, honestly and enthusiastically complimentary, and she was encouraged to reach higher in her aspirations.

Soon she had the lead soprano's role in Mexico City's renowned Les Belles Artes Opera Company's production of *Manon Lescaut*, the first American soprano ever to have a lead roll in the company's twenty-five-year history. On opening night, the 6,000-seat house was sold out. In the audience were many dignitaries, including the American ambassador to Mexico. When the curtain

Annette, in full costume, playing the lead role in "Manon Lescault."

fell at the end, there were standing ovations for the lead tenor and Annette, with many cries of Bravo! and Brava! Dick was so proud of her performance, she says, that when he came backstage to congratulate her he had tears in his eyes. It was the only time she ever saw tears in his eyes.

It was the biggest night of her life as a performer. The reviews in the paper the next day were smashing. The critics raved. "Annette Martin was Manon!" they proclaimed. They said that her voice was "lilting and lovely," and that she gave "a bravura performance." Annette was aglow.

Visitors in the Night

Since she was not doing psychic readings, Annette had shut down the psychic view screen in her mind. Occasionally she'd have flashes, but she'd mostly ignore them.

But then strange things began to happen.

One night Annette awoke to the sound of a familiar voice calling her out of a sound sleep. She got up and walked through the living room on the cold, stone floor to the heavy, wooden front door and pulled on the hefty, iron door latch.

A white mist drifted across the courtyard in front of the condo, covering their car parked in the driveway. The mist turned gray and solidified into the figure of a woman.

Annette felt the eerie chill she'd felt when Henry Holt's ghost had appeared to her in Hong Kong. She remembers thinking, Oh, no, here we go again...

The figure said: "Annette, come closer."

Annette stepped out onto the front steps and into the cool night air. She could barely make out the features of someone quite familiar.

"I couldn't leave without saying good-bye to you," the figure said. "I know this is a surprise, but my body has been riddled with cancer. I just couldn't hold on any longer."

Annette then recognized her. The voice, the features of her face: it was her neighbor, Betty, from back in Saratoga, California. She was dressed in her usual, baggy jeans. She had long, straight, brown hair, blown by the wind. "I didn't mean to startle you, Annette. I've come to thank you for all the company you gave me while you were living in California. You made me laugh and cry. I so missed you when you left."

Annette remembers that at that moment she couldn't utter a sound. She was greatly saddened. Betty had been a warm friend, helpful, loyal, easy-going; they shared a love of gardening. It took Annette a moment to fully realize that Betty was an apparition. Even though she had had a similar visit from Henry Holt's ghost, seeing Betty and realizing she was dead was deeply disturbing to Annette.

"Betty, good-bye..." was all Annette could manage.

Betty waved and, with that, faded into the night.

A moment later: "Honey, who is at the door?" Dick called from the bedroom. "Who are you talking to?"

She told him who it was and said Betty wanted to say good-bye. Dick could see Annette was shaken. He held her for a long time.

A Visitor in Trouble

The next morning Annette and Dick told the boys about the ghostly visit. The boys thought it was cool that Mom was able to see and talk to ghosts.

The following night she had another visitor.

She heard a boy's voice calling her: "Please help me! I don't want to die! I'm afraid, but I can't hold on!"

She sat up in bed. "Who are you?"

Slowly, the gray mist appeared at the foot of the bed and the figure of a boy emerged in the now familiar, semi-solid form. He was about sixteen with light-blond hair.

Annette squinted at him. "Are you a friend of my son, Scott?" she asked.

"No," he said. "I'm Shannon. Shannon, the son of David and Sherry. I know you can see me. Can you help me? I'm dying! Please, I don't want to die!"

She could see he had blood cancer.

"If it's your time, there's nothing I can do," she said.

"Help me, I'm so scared."

"All I can do is send you some White Light to help you get to the other side."

She closed her eyes and took her three deep breaths and visualized the White Light shining on the boy. After a few moments, she opened her eyes and he was gone.

The next morning, after a fitful night's sleep, Annette searched through her things for her California address book. She finally managed to find it and put a call through to David and Sherry in California. Yes, Shannon had died of leukemia early that morning.

She told them about the ghostly visit. There was a silence for a moment. "Yes, Annette," Sherry said, crying. "He told us he saw a blond woman and she had given him some beautiful White Light to help him go to the other side...We thought he was delirious. We had no idea it was you! He said everything would be fine, and he was no longer afraid to die. He passed away moments later," she said between sobs. "He passed away with a smile on his face. Thank you, Annette, for being there and assisting him. We felt so damn helpless."

Annette told them how sorry she was that they had lost their son, but she was so glad she could help.

This was the only time, Annette says, that someone in the throes of death came to ask her for help. The Gift has its price, but it has its rewards as well. Helping to ease Shannon's terror of dying was one of the biggest joys in her life as a psychic.

Another Night-time Visitor

A few nights later, Annette was awakened again by a voice calling her name. It was a male voice.

God, she thought, not another one.

She went to the front door and found the mist forming into the figure of a man. He was an old man, stooped, thin, frail.

"You probably don't remember me, Annette, but my name is Joseph Cox. We met a few times back in California."

She searched her memory; she couldn't recall his name. He didn't look at all familiar.

"What do you want, Mr. Cox?" she said.

"I just wanted to say good-bye to someone and you were on the way, so I stopped by."

And with that, he disappeared into the night.

She closed the door. Was she becoming a stop on the railroad to the afterlife? she mused.

She wished Mr. Cox well on his journey and went back to bed.

Dick, who, as mentioned earlier, had come from a family that belonged to the Vedanta religion and was involved with seances in his home, was tolerant of this ghostly business, but these visits interrupted Annette's sleep—and his. "Perhaps," he said, "you ought to let these ghosts know there is nothing you can do…and you certainly don't need to say good-bye to everyone who is passing on to the afterlife."

She said he had a point. But there was no visit the next night, or the next, and she thought perhaps she was no longer a stop on the way to eternity.

But then the following Saturday, Annette was called out of a sound sleep by a wispy, woman's voice:

"Annette, Annette…"

Annette sat up. The voice grew stronger. "Annette… Annette…"

Again, she felt the same eerie chill.

She got up and went to the front door and opened it and stepped out. Within seconds the white mist swirled and darkened and the figure of a young woman in her early twenties formed before her eyes.

"You don't know me well, Annette," she said, "but we met at a conference. You were so sweet and kind to me, giving me a very accurate reading later that evening. I have had a fatal accident in my car, but I wanted to say thank you before I left."

Annette said she was welcome and the apparition vanished. She did remember the woman, but only vaguely.

She went back inside. Dick was right; this had to stop.

The next morning she mediated and asked the souls of the dearly departed to visit during the day instead of at night.

It did the trick, she says. Thereafter, she says, she received no more good-bye visits from the dead, day or night.

In the middle of August, Dick came home one night, beaming. He'd been promoted again. He was going back to Fairchild as the general manager of the Hong Kong plant.

Annette hated to leave the Mexico Opera and the wonderful singers and directors, but she wouldn't miss the traffic congestion, the crowds, the smog, or the mañana attitude.

She started packing that very night.

Welcome Back to Hong Kong

Annette and Dick and the two kids stayed first at Annette's favorite hangout in all the world: the Repulse Bay Hotel. Their suite had fourteen-foot ceilings and a fine, old sitting room with overstuffed chairs and Victorian mahogany tables, brass table lamps, and a Tiffany chandelier. Annette found it delightful for relaxing, or reading, or having friends over. The boys, she remembers, loved their stay in the hotel. They could walk to school and then go right down to the beach in the afternoon and play in the sand, swim, fool around.

Annette resumed going to yoga classes at the hotel with her friend Faye. She and Faye took up their automatic writing sessions again and soon Annette was doing readings for medical clients. To her amazement, she found she was delighted to be doing readings again after her long vacation from them while she'd been in Mexico. She was careful to keep a schedule and not let herself become overwhelmed.

One afternoon she started having strange "flashes," and then she had a vision. She "saw" her Aunt Floydee, who lived in San Francisco, falling out of a hospital bed onto the floor, saw a black-and-blue lump on her right arm from the fall, and saw she had a concussion on the right side of her brain and a small tumor on her right ovary. Oh, my God, she thought, aren't they taking care of her?

She called her mother the next morning. Yes, indeed, Aunt Floydee had taken two falls out of the bed, and yes, she had a bruise and a concussion. At Annette's request, they checked her for a tumor and found that she did have a small tumor, but because of her age and condition they were not going to operate, so Annette didn't have to worry.

The family soon moved into a recently renovated 2,500-square-foot flat with two servants' quarters. They hired a wonderful Shanghai cook, Shou, who was once a professor in China and recently worked as a chef on one of the big steamers that went up-river into China. He was tall and thin, and he spoke good English. They also hired a house boy (called then a "wash"), Amah, whom the family called "Mae." He was a short butterball of a man, sweet, kind, and motherly toward the whole family.

Soon both Annette and Dick were singing for the Hong Kong Singers. They were the two leads in *The Merry Widow*, and did ten performances with the Hong Kong Symphony. The performances drew packed houses and rave reviews. Several Hong Kong Singers concerts followed, and another performance with the Hong Kong Symphony.

Annette answered a notice for a tryout for an American actress who could do ingenue roles for voice-overs for a Hong Kong film production company. She was hired on the spot.

She thought something was strange when they had her take a cab to a certain corner, where a car picked her up and left her at another corner, where she got a cab to a secret location in a seedy apartment building. Apparently the producers wanted to keep their location secret, but why, Annette had not a clue. It turned out that the movies they were making were called "blue movies." They might have been a little racy in the 1950s, but this was the 1970s. They would be rated PG–13 now.

She enjoyed doing the voice-overs, which included five full-length movies. The other voices were supplied by British actors faking incredibly bad American accents.

Again Annette was busy with entertaining and showing visitors around and going to antique shops looking for Mandarin sleeves to add to her collection. As the general manager's wife, she was supposed to make sure the families of the ex-pat executives were taken care of. Several of the corporate wives in Annette's circle of friends were having trouble adjusting to life in Hong Kong and she spent a lot of time trying to help them relieve the strain on their marriages.

Annette and Dick bought a twenty-eight-foot motor boat, "Mrs. Hooper," and hired a boat boy to live aboard because the boat people would strip it if left unattended. On Sundays Annette and Dick would take a few guests to Lantau Island with a small flotilla of boats for a picnic. She remembers being on the water as a spectacular experience, watching the junks go by with their colorful, deep-red and yellow sails, laundry hanging all over them, children waving.

At the other end of the lagoon there would be a few sampans tied together, covered with tents of brightly colored material—a floating brothel. The customers would be brought out in sampans or in small motor launches. The Wan Chia section of Hong Kong was an enormous red-light district. The U.S. Seventh Fleet and the British Navy supplied the customer base.

During the following year the family took a lot of trips: Bali, India, Nepal, Indonesia, Singapore, the Seychelle Islands, and Africa, where they went on safari. It was an exciting time.

Annette was enjoying life in Hong Kong once again.

But their stay abruptly came to an end in 1975 when Dick was appointed general manager of the Fairchild plant in San Rafael, California.

They were going home at last. Annette knew she was about to have some big changes in her life. Some of these changes would open up her professional life to new challenges and opportunities. But in her personal life, she sensed there were dark clouds forming on the horizon.

Chapter Seven

California, Here We Come

Ray Worring (the private detective and writer we met on the Cottonwood case; see Chapter One) visited Annette one day in the fall of 1998 to interview her for a book he was co-writing, Psychic Criminology. At the end of the interview he asked her for a reading, just for the experience. He said as far as he knew he was in perfect health and had no symptoms of illness of any kind. He wrote the following letter to Annette a few months later:

> *Dear Annette:*
> *You might be interested to know when we saw you last, you said I had a kidney difficulty in a reading. You drew my left kidney and said I should see the doctor right away. Well, they removed it last November.* [The kidney was cancerous. Annette's early warning saved his life.] *I'm doing fine now. You helped inspire my book. Thank you.*

The following is a transcript from Annette's "Your Psychic World" live radio show:

> *Annette, this is Bernadette, the woman you told to go and see her doctor because you felt there was a heart problem. I want to thank you for being so persistent with me. I didn't want to believe that there could be anything wrong with my heart and did not go to my doctor. But when I attended the health fair a little voice kept saying, "Listen to what Annette said and have an EKG, just to make sure." I did have a problem and since I've had an operation to fix a bad heart valve. Thank you for saving*

*my life! I know that I never would have gone and had the EKG if you
hadn't read me that night. You are truly wonderful!*

Once back in the states, Annette and her family set up a temporary
household in a rented house in Marin County, across the Golden Gate
Bridge from San Francisco, while Annette and Dick searched to buy a
new home. They finally found one in the new suburban community of
Wild Horse Valley in Novato, about thirty miles north of San Francisco.

This was a spacious, 3,500-square-foot home with four bedrooms
and three baths. The landscaping was complete and the living room had
a massive fireplace and floor-to-ceiling windows on two walls that looked
onto a tree-lined courtyard. They got their grand piano out of storage.
Annette thought it looked elegant in the large, white-carpeted living
room. There was a spacious game room and, out in back, a magnificent
swimming pool, all on a half-acre lot, where Annette figured she could
create a wonderful garden. They needed such a large home because they
would be doing a lot of entertaining, which was expected of the general
manager of the vast Fairchild Semiconductors facility.

One thing Annette missed from her days of living overseas was the
household staff; it was back to reality, and that came, she says, as a shock.

The boys were enrolled in school. Scott, the younger, went to a
public middle school not far from home, and Craig was enrolled in Marin
Academy, a private high school in San Rafael that was just a few blocks
from the Fairchild plant. Dick could drop Craig off at school on his way
to work, which was great.

Life returned to normal.

Annette Meets Old Friends

One morning Annette went for a stroll, taking in the new neighborhood. It was late spring and the surrounding hills were turning from
green to golden brown under the California sun. Hawks circled over-
head. Despite the fact that she no longer had a household staff, she was
glad to be back in California, to be home. Suddenly she heard a voice:

"Annette! Annette De La Roche!"

She turned to see a thin, dark-haired woman standing in the front
doorway of a house. Annette couldn't quite make out the face, but the
voice was familiar. It turned out to be a woman named Franny, who had

been a close friend in high school and a neighbor when they were girls! They had gone to Abraham Lincoln High School in San Francisco together. They chatted for a while and Annette learned that another classmate, Nancy, lived in the next street. What luck, Annette thought, to move in and have old friends nearby. Shazam!

When the three got together they chatted about old times. Annette figured she'd better get it over with; she told them about her work as a psychic. She was delighted to find that they both seemed fascinated. Franny, with a wink, said she was not in the least surprised.

Later, at home, Dick was excited to find that Annette had old friends in the neighborhood. Since he was a sociable guy, he suggested that Annette invite Franny and Nancy and their families over for dinner. Great idea, Annette said, and set about to make the arrangements.

The night of the dinner party, Franny and Larry, her husband, arrived first with their two boys; introductions were made and drinks were served. Craig and Scott took the boys into the backyard to toss baseballs in the cool of the evening.

Later that evening, when the conversation got around to what was going on in the neighborhood, Nancy told Annette about a psychiatrist she knew, Dr. Gerald Jampolsky, who was doing wonderful things to aid cancer patients, using hypnosis, meditation, biofeedback, and visualization techniques. He had an interest in psychic phenomena, she said, and would probably like to meet her. Annette said she'd like to meet him, too. She had always had a desire to have her work validated by the medical profession and this might be her chance.

A meeting was arranged at Dr. Jampolsky's office in Tiburon, a quaint little town on San Francisco Bay, north of San Francisco and the Golden Gate Bridge.

Annette and the Shrink

Annette was a little nervous about meeting Dr. Jampolsky. After all, he was a renowned psychiatrist. Annette knew medical people usually turned up their snobby noses at the very idea of psychic phenomena, but on Nancy's assurance that Dr. Jampolsky would be open-minded, Annette went to the appointment feeling optimistic. What the hey, he was interested in the effect of attitude on healing and other "new age" ideas.

When she arrived at Dr. Jampolsky's office on the boardwalk in Tiburon—a trendy, rather rustic row of offices and shops and restaurants—Annette thought this fit with what she'd expected. Inside, the office was nicely appointed in leather furniture with brass lamps and a few ferns, as one would expect in a psychiatrist's office. He had, she recalls, a large, beautiful oak desk. In a way, she found the traditional furnishings reassuring. He had a wall full of degrees, including one from Stanford Medical School.

Then she met the man himself. He was thin and about five-foot-ten, with a narrow face and a pleasant smile. He had the reserved, aloof demeanor one would expect of a mental health professional, and he didn't at all seem like the hippie doc riding the tide of the New Age, as some people had described him. He was rather pale, and Annette sensed he must have had a severe alcohol problem at one time.

Dr. Jampolsky seemed to have a great curiosity about her and a keen interest in her, which pleased Annette. She wondered if he thought she was a rare and interesting fruitcake. He started out by asking her about her childhood, who her parents were, where she lived while growing up, how her parents got along…

With each answer, he would nod and take notes, pausing at times to consider her answer before he'd move on to the next question. She felt like a patient being analyzed, but she stuck with it. She was as curious about him as he was about her.

She told Dr. Jampolsky about the White Light and her spirit guide, Cama, and how she got advice from Edgar Cayce; she told him about her trances and what she "saw" inside people's bodies.

She sensed he was incredulous, but he kept right on asking questions. When he was through with digging into her background, he started asking about her cosmological views: how she felt about God, where man came from, did she hear voices, was Cama an angel, what did she think heaven was like? She didn't quite understand the purpose of all his questions and when she'd ask, he was evasive and promised it would all become clear to her.

She met with him on more than half a dozen occasions for an hour at a time. He even interviewed her parents. She wondered if he thought she might be deranged.

Finally, he asked her what she saw for him. She blinked. What? He wanted her to do a reading of him? This flabbergasted her. Was this some kind of test, or did he really want to know? He smiled his enigmatic little smile and asked her to please do it.

She closed her eyes, took three deep breaths, and when she opened her eyes, she said: "Dr. Jampolsky, you are going to open some kind of center or school. There will be many people involved with this project and it will be very successful."

He scoffed, gesturing a big NO with a wave of his hand.

"And," she went on, "you're going to write many books that will be widely read."

He shook his head. "Not possible," he said. "I have no time to write books, and I'm certainly not going to open this center or whatever it is. You are definitely wrong there."

She smiled. "We'll see, won't we?" she said. "And I don't think we'll have long to wait."

At the next session he started asking Annette questions and she stopped him. "Look, Dr. Jampolsky, either you think I'm schizophrenic or nutso or something. I have to know why you keep asking me all these questions."

He put down his pen and looked at her over the top of his glasses. "I don't think you're schizophrenic at all. In fact, I think you have a fascinating mind."

"Then what are we doing here?"

"I would like you to work with some patients of mine."

Shazam!

This was her chance. This was what she was hoping for all her life: to be tested fairly, to be recognized by the medical community!

She said it was a great idea; she'd love to demonstrate how she did what she did. It would be a chance for her to help a whole lot more people if the doctors were on her side. And it would mean she'd have scientific validation for her work.

It turned out that Dr. Jampolsky was working with very sick patients. He was trying to help them physically by alleviating their terror and depression without using drugs. He had a strong belief that a positive attitude could help a patient either in their recovery or to ease their suffering in dying.

He wanted Annette to do a reading of a patient for him as a test. She agreed. He wanted her to read not just this patient's physical condition, but her psychological problems as well. "Can you do that?" he asked.

"Yes," she said.

Annette Takes a Test

The patient turned out to be a woman in her sixties, a polite, reserved matron with a skeptical look on her face. Her name was Thea.

After the social amenities were observed and Annette explained what she was going to do, she took three deep breaths and went into a trance for a few moments, then she opened her eyes and said, "Thea, you have a small tumor in your left breast."

The woman flushed, but said nothing. Dr. Jampolsky looked surprised. Annette figured she must be correct.

"The result of the biopsy is not in as yet," Dr. Jampolsky said. "But there is a lump."

"I'm afraid she'll have to have a mastectomy," Annette said, "but she'll have a good recovery and the cancer will not return."

The woman smiled a nervous little smile.

Annette went on: "You also have an iron deficiency and are tired, especially in the afternoon and evening. Generally, you're in very good shape. I suggest a firmer mattress for you lower back."

Thea nodded.

"And the psychological?" Dr. Jampolsky asked.

Annette closed her eyes for a moment, then said: "You have had several husbands—three, I think, and you're not getting on well with the current one. Your problem is you loved your father who died on you when you were a girl and you never forgave him. Your love soured and turned to hate. The hatred you have for your father, you put on your husbands. You're short-tempered and often find yourself crying for no reason. The reason is you never got over the loss of your father—Oh, my God! He committed suicide, didn't he?"

Thea teared up, nodding.

"And somehow you blame yourself. It had nothing to do with you— he had problems with his business. Was he stealing from his company?"

She nodded.

"It really had nothing to do with you at all. He didn't want to go to jail; that's all there was to it."

She was weeping now. "But if he really loved me, how could he have done it?"

"He was in terror of confinement and the disgrace. He wanted to spare you and your mother the ordeal of a trial."

"Yes, I see. I see. He did care for us."

"He cared very much."

Annette glanced at Dr. Jampolsky. His mouth was open in astonishment.

"That's all I'm getting," Annette said.

Thea grabbed Annette's hand. "Thank you, thank you, thank you! I'm going to be better with George—he's my husband. You'll see. He's really a very good man who tries very hard. I've been just terrible to him."

Annette leaned over, touching Thea's arm and said, "Have that surgery as soon as you can, promise?"

"I promise."

Annette reassured her, "You're going to be fine."

"I know I am," she said.

Dr. Jampolsky Has an Idea

After Thea had left, Dr. Jampolsky collapsed in a chair. "I'm overwhelmed," he said. "The way she opened up to you—it was amazing, Annette."

"Now when are you going to open that center and start writing books?"

He put his sober face back on and shook his head. "Never, and never." He was thoughtful for a moment, and then he said, "I have a few arrangements to make, Annette, then I'd like you to come and do some readings for some colleagues of mine. Would that be all right?"

Annette felt a little knot of fear forming. Okay, doing a reading for Dr. Jampolsky was one thing, but for a bunch of strangers with MDs after their names, that was something else.

"Look, Annette," he said, "I want to show that there is more to the mind than what doctors know. I want to show them that we should be examining those aspects."

For Annette, this was a momentous step. She'd barely gotten used to Dr. Jampolsky; he made her plenty uptight with his million questions. This was all so new to her, but she remembered that day long ago when she was eleven and she saw the long line of people and Cama's voice telling her these were the people she was supposed to help. Well…here was the way to reach them.

She found herself nodding her assent.

"All right, I'll set it up," he said.

Annette vs. the Doctors

A few days went by, then a week, then a month, and nothing happened. Annette thought Dr. Jampolsky might have decided against it, or he hadn't been able to drum up any interest. Finally, he called and asked her to come to San Rafael. He asked whether she would mind if he videotaped the session. "Not at all," she replied bravely.

Annette arrived with her friend and volunteer secretary, June Rucker. The event was held in a former junior high school—now a community center—at ten in the morning. The videotape of the session has been lost, but June Rucker took careful, detailed notes, from which the following account is drawn. The date was December 10, 1975, two days after Annette's thirty-seventh birthday.

Annette, feeling nervous and jittery, and June, confident and reassuring, went up the front stairs and were greeted by a young man who ushered them into what used to be a classroom. They could hear voices echoing down the cold corridors, but they didn't see anyone else. They sat there for a while until Dr. Jampolsky arrived. He seemed to have an edge to his usually cool demeanor, like a nervous host at a dinner party. He gave Annette a hug and said, "Just relax, we're getting set up. I'll be back for you in a few minutes."

Annette began pacing the floor. She didn't know what to expect. Maybe they'd be downright hostile. Maybe she wouldn't be able to concentrate, maybe she'd lose her nerve, maybe she'd stutter and stammer and look ridiculous.

Suddenly visions started coming to her. She went to the blackboard and started drawing circles. "There is a problem with the bladder and filtering system," Annette blurted out. June snatched her notebook from her purse and started scribbling notes. "Who are we talking about?" she asked.

"The patient they want me to do a reading for, of course," Annette answered.

"But where is she?" June asked.

"Nearby," Annette said.

At that moment, Dr. Jampolsky returned. "Annette, what are you doing? Wait, don't start—the panel is in the other room with the patient."

"Oh...of course. I guess I'm a little jumpy."

Dr. Jampolsky took Annette by the hand and ushered her down a maze of hallways to a large meeting room. She took a deep breath as she entered. A long table was situated on the opposite side of the room. There sat thirteen doctors, and none of them were smiling.

Annette gulped. A few colleagues, didn't he say? There were three women and ten men on the panel, most in their thirties or forties, but some older. One of the men had a full, bushy, white beard; another wore a goatee. A few had their arms folded across their chests. They were all staring at her, looking about as open-minded as tree stumps.

Two cameramen stood by, manning a large video camera.

Dr. Jampolsky introduced Annette as "Mrs. Martin," who, he said, "is here to give us a demonstration of her skills as a medical intuitive." He showed her to a chair beside a small table. June sat next to her and handed Annette her yellow tablet and a pencil.

A young woman, thin, frail, and looking as frightened as a deer caught in the headlights of a beer truck, was seated by herself between Annette and the panel. Annette asked her if she was the patient, even though she already knew she was.

"Yes, I am."

"And your first name?"

"Dorothy."

"I'm Annette, how do you do?"

Dr. Jampolsky introduced one of the doctors as Dr. Munroe and said he was the patient's physician. He told Annette she could begin whenever she was ready.

The cameramen started taping. Annette let out three deep breaths and slid into a trance. Her hand with the pencil in it started moving over the tablet. The following is taken from June Rucker's transcript:

[*Annette pauses, closes her eyes, her hand moves quickly across the pad.*]

JUNE: What are you seeing, Annette?

ANNETTE: Oh, the whole left side. Dorothy, I see you sitting…Wait! There's something that's severed!

DOROTHY: Yes.

ANNETTE: Between the waist and the tip of the spine, ah [*sighs*]. There's a severing, ah, is this true?

DOROTHY: Yes.

ANNETTE: I don't see any motion, paralysis, no movement…[*Annette pauses again, trembling at what she's seeing. She chokes back a sob*] You will have to excuse my emotional outbursts. [*Annette is crying*] I don't see any movement; I see a paralysis…No movement, no movement!

DOROTHY: Yes.

ANNETTE: There has been a severing in the back with fractures along the spine and there is also a hearing problem.
[*Deep breath*] I see an automobile hitting a wall, and then
a loud noise like a crash! You were pinned inside the car,
Dorothy!

DR. JAMPOLSKY: So what you are saying is that there has been
an automobile accident that caused the paralysis; she has
been left with a paralysis and a fracture?

ANNETTE: Yes, that is what I see, an automobile accident.

DR. SUTTER: And a hearing problem?

ANNETTE: Yes. And oh, this blood, it's not filtering properly.
Is this where the kidneys are? Are they together?

DR. JAMPOLSKY: I should say at this point that Annette does
not understand anatomy, so she has been working with
June who is a nurse. If there are any questions about the
anatomy, I would like to help as much as I can.

ANNETTE: All right. I see two [anatomical] things together.
They seem to be working together. [*Annette draws two ob-
long shapes on the yellow pad*] Are these the kidneys?

DR. JAMPOLSKY [*looking*]: It can be. In other words, both the
kidneys and liver are filtering the system. There is one
liver and two kidneys.

ANNETTE: Yes, I see two pulsating together. Do they work
together? Do they have the same motion together? Is the
motion the same?

DR. JAMPOLSKY: I'd say no. They work at their own rate. A
different motion.

ANNETTE: Is the kidney close to the liver?

DR. JAMPOLSKY: Yes.

ANNETTE: On the right-hand side?

DR. JAMPOLSKY: Yes.

ANNETTE: The filtering system is not working properly. We
are getting blood, very dark.

JUNE: Is this what you were seeing, Annette, in the other room?

ANNETTE: Yes! The filtering system! Dorothy, is your urine dark?

DOROTHY: Yes, at times, if I have not had enough to drink.

ANNETTE: You must force the liquid down; drink a lot of

water to help the kidneys, because your filtering system is not working properly, OK, due to inactivity. I feel another pain further down, further down in the back, here. Is there such a pain here, [*pointing*] too?

DOROTHY: Yes.

ANNETTE [*to the panel*]: She is in a lot of pain, the whole spinal cord! What I believe Dorothy must do now is, she has a lot of tension and stress, a tremendous amount of tension. It must be eliminated! Dorothy, you must try very hard to eliminate this. When the stress and strain are gone, the pain will melt away. It won't be a cure, but you will be able to go on. Do you understand what I am talking about? The more tension and stress builds up, the more it tightens every single muscle along the spinal cord and you have to relax those. And the muscles will relax and the pain will go away and resolve itself.

DR. JAMPOLSKY: If she were to go to a doctor, what would be her main concern? What would the doctor say her chief complaint was? Annette, can we get some help on what might be causing the pain besides the tension and stress that you just described? I don't know whether it's something we can see but it might play a part in the causation of pain.

ANNETTE: Yes, umm…

DR. JAMPOLSKY: I'd like to say, Annette, that one of the reasons I like working with you is that I feel that we who are working in the medical profession sometimes are not able to come up with a diagnosis. We have to spend a lot of money on a lot of examinations, and I feel there is a valid role for psychics such as you to have available as a paramedical person when we have some diagnosis problem. This is one of the reasons in the interest I have. This is a problem. I am interested in what you might have to say about that.

ANNETTE: Yes, Dr. Jampolsky, as you were talking, I have to show you a few things. [*Ignoring Dr. Jampolsky's academic question, Annette continues drawing a picture on the yellow tablet*] Uhm, these are the lungs? I see a white line. While you were talking, I kept seeing a white line. Okay, we have here the lungs, [*pointing to picture she drew on pad*] I am feeling it on my right side. I see a white line on my right. [*Turning towards Dorothy*] Dorothy, I see things like an x-ray, which are black and white, most of the time. Sometimes I see color, but most of the time it is black and white. In this particular case I see a white line. Do you cough a lot?

DOROTHY: No.

DR. MOORE [*one of the doctors on the panel*]: Does this white line indicate to you an interruption? Would you like some feedback on that?

ANNETTE: Yes.

DR. MOORE: Is there any evidence on an x-ray [*turning towards Dorothy*]?

ANNETTE: Yes or no, Dorothy?

DOROTHY: No! [*Something must have touched a nerve; she's suddenly upset*].

DR. JAMPOLSKY: All right, for a moment I am going to take you to another area. Let's go to the personality.

DOROTHY: You know, I do have a pain there!

ANNETTE: It's like a line?

DOROTHY: It goes right across here [*Dorothy draws her hand across her back, in the exact place that Annette is describing*].

DR. JAMPOLSKY: I wonder if we could go to another area, and that is the area of personality. Could you give us her personality traits?

DR. SUTTER: Ask how does she feel today, currently, rather than to complicate it by including the past or in your words, is it better to concentrate on the past?

ANNETTE: A lot of it is right here today.

DR. SUTTER: Now would you describe the type of person Dorothy is? How she feels much of the time? How she relates with other people, relatives, friends, and coworkers? And her feelings in different situations?

ANNETTE: I am feeling a very introverted personality. Fear, many fears of everything, and a great deal of anxiety.

DR. SUTTER: That is as specific as I get too. I didn't probe any further than that. How do you feel she handles anger? Or is there much anger? How is it handled? Anger as an important component in her daily existence?

ANNETTE: I see a red spot, which symbolizes anger. I don't feel anger all the time with Dorothy. There is anger and...sometimes it comes out, bang! But not very often...This is why we have so much stress in the back. Dorothy, do you put it all inside of you?

DOROTHY: I don't know!

DR. JAMPOLSKY: It is my impression in working with Dorothy that, in my opinion, that is a very valid statement.

ANNETTE: All right.

DR. SUTTER: Dorothy did write on this form that she does tend to keep her feelings to herself. Now whether she keeps her anger to herself is something else again, but feelings are kept to herself. How about her relationships with other people?

ANNETTE: Cautious, withdrawn.

DR. SUTTER: Parents, children, friends?

ANNETTE: The same.

[*Dorothy is obviously agitated*]

DR. JAMPOLSKY: I see our time is runnings out. I think we should give more feedback.

ANNETTE: You are having a lot of pain right now, at this moment.

DOROTHY: Yes.

DR. LITTELL: How about the hearing, Dr. Jampolsky?

DR. JAMPOLSKY: There is a very definite problem with hearing.

DOROTHY: That happened when I was twelve years old, a mastoid or meningitis infection and it popped, liquid came out and I lost my balance.

DR. JAMPOLSKY [*to the panel*]: I would like to give you some background now. Dorothy was involved in a very serious automobile accident on Mount Tamalpais. She was under the influence of alcohol. She has had a lot of fractures. Since then she has been in many hospitals, indeed she had many fractures from the accident, indeed a foot drop and with a diagnosis of paralysis. Her main problem has been that of pain. She has other types of problems, an infection with her foot and there seems to be another problem in urination and metabolic problems. [*to Annette*] At least, in my judgment, you have never seen Dorothy before, Annette, and you started working on the diagnosis before you actually came into the room, locating some of the symptoms; this would indicate that you are in tune in a very interesting way. Dr. Ruth Sutter, could you give us some feedback on Annette's impressions and how accurate she was?

DR. SUTTER: I think that your feelings, Annette, regarding her temperament are quite accurate and in keeping with her current assessment of herself. The tension and the mode of handling anger, the degree of anger. Those are certainly accurate there. Of being a quiet person, feeling much frustration, those certainly do match with her written reports here.

DR. JAMPOLSKY: I am going to ask Dorothy how accurate you think Annette was tonight? You've never met Annette before. Can you give a percentage of her accuracy, 1-100, of your physical diagnosis? Would you say 50 percent, 80 percent, 100 percent accurate?

DOROTHY: 35 percent.

This ends the transcript.

Annette was stunned by the 35 percent estimate. It was obvious she was closer to 100 percent. Annette figured she must have hit a sensitive spot while reading Dorothy's personality.

At this point Dr. Jampolsky turned to the other doctors and shrugged his shoulders in disbelief. It was apparent to all of them the accuracy was much, much higher, but there was no point in arguing about it.

Dr. Jampolsky: Thank you, Dorothy. You were beautiful, Annette.

And so, she thought, was Edgar Cayce, who had been comforting and encouraging her all along, and helping her with the diagnosis.

She did two more cases that day, and when it was all over the doctors judged she was 90-95 percent accurate.

Annette had her validation.

Follow-up on Dorothy, One Year Later

Annette got a call a year later from Dorothy's sister. She asked Annette if she recalled what she'd said about Dorothy's condition.

Annette replied, "Only vaguely." She did recall that Dorothy was paralyzed.

"I meant about her kidneys."

"Oh, yes."

"You said there was something wrong with her filtering system."

"Ah, yes. Now I remember. Did they find out anything?"

"Well, three months ago, we put her in the hospital with gangrene in her foot. She looked like she was dying. They wanted to amputate! I went crazy and called an internist. You know what? He found a bladder infection, one like they'd never seen before. She had had it for a long time and I can't imagine that they didn't discover it earlier. Annette, I told them what you had told the doctors and they didn't listen!"

This was nothing new to Annette, but it was always good to hear. She thanked the woman and wished Dorothy well.

Annette Spreads the White Light Around

True to Annette's prediction, Dr. Jampolsky opened his Center for Attitudinal Healing. At the center, he formed a support group for children with cancer, a place where they could come and have a safe environment to express their deepest feelings and fears and find some peace. He said he wanted a place where children could learn to choose love over fear. He had a vision, he said, of "a place not only of loss and grief, but a place where both children and adults could learn to live fully each moment and bring healing relationships into all parts of their lives." Annette thought this was a marvelous idea and went to work for him as an unpaid volunteer.

To begin, Dr. Jampolsky wanted Annette to teach children how to meditate, and at the same time he wanted her to show doctors and nurses how to develop their psychic abilities.

"Can do," she said.

Over the next few months Annette carefully planned her program—with the advice of her two "faithful companions" as she calls them, Cama and Edgar Cayce. Early in 1976 she began with a class of half a dozen kids with cancer, who were undergoing chemotherapy and radiation treatments that made them weak and nauseated. She had them lie on the floor and guided their mediations, journeys in their minds through beautiful gardens, parks, and mountains. She had them fly across oceans and visit magical lands and meet magical beings.

She taught them how to breathe deeply through their noses and exhale through their mouths and how to visualize the White Light.

After a few sessions, she remembers, they'd come through the doorway smiling and happy. At least for a while, they could leave planet Earth and their suffering behind them.

Dr. Jampolsky was thrilled with the results Annette was getting. And so were the kids' doctors and parents.

Annette then started a class in the evening for health-care professionals. At her first class she told them their lives would never be the same after they had taken the class, and this prediction was proved correct time and time again.

By the second class, she had them sending pictures to a partner by way of telepathy and the members of the class were astounded by the phenomenal results. She told them they were intuitive all along and just didn't know it. How many times, she asked, did they just "know" what was wrong with a patient before a single test was taken? They all agreed that they very often knew even though they had no clue how they knew. Their guesses were much better than chance would predict. One said he and many of his colleagues were correct in their subjective diagnosis 99 percent of the time.

Annette felt that her job was to teach them to tune in to their already highly-developed intuitive sense.

During the sixth session, one of the nurses said she sensed something wrong with one of her patients who had come in for some tests for chest pains. She called the attending physician and he asked for the man's vital signs, which were fine. The doctor said he'd be down to see the patient in the morning, but the nurse insisted he come immediately— there was definitely something wrong. The doctor was irritated with her, but he finally caved in and said he would be there in ten minutes.

By the time he got there the patient was already going into shock; his gall bladder was rupturing. They were able to get the man prepped and into surgery in time; the surgery was successful and the patient recovered fully.

Thanks to Annette's counseling, the nurse's intuition had saved the patient's life!

Annette was pleased with her work and in the future she'd do more teaching at San Andreas Health Council in Palo Alto; Foothill College in Los Altos, California; Stanford University; the University of Hawaii—as well as at innumerable private classes in homes and at her office suite in Campbell, California. This work would lead her eventually to write *Discovering Your Psychic World,* which was first published in 1994 and is still in print, available at most bookstores or at Amazon.com.

Annette's prediction about Dr. Jampolsky becoming an author also soon came true. His first best-selling, self-help book, *Love is Letting Go of Fear* was published in 1979 and now is considered something of a classic in the field. He would go on to write several other books, including *Teach Only Love, The 12 Principles of Attitudinal Healing, Good-bye to Guilt, Out of Darkness into the Light, One Person Can Make a Difference,* and others.

The Center for Attitudinal Healing, which Annette helped to launch, has spawned over 150 independent programs and centers around the globe, serving schools, prisons, medical centers, and the corporate world, in both the developed countries and developing countries, including active war zones.

Chapter Eight

Annette Sees a Body

Annette "read" some of my antique photos from the Old West and picked up on many of my Jesse James photos. She told me that Jesse was a womanizer, very adept at convincing people of whatever he wanted, enjoyed pulling the wool over people, and liked impersonating different kinds of professions, even going so far as to dress up as a woman. She also said that Jesse James did not die as history said. She said he lived the rest of his life out West in a mountainous area like Colorado or thereabouts. He lived with an Indian woman who buried him some time around the turn of the century. His true grave will never be found. I believe this all to be true.

—Ben Taylor

Editor's note:

The official account of the death of Jesse James is that while hanging a picture in his home he was shot in the back by his one of his gang members, a distant cousin, Robert Ford, in Saint Joseph, Missouri, on April 3, 1882. Ford was paid a $10,000 reward by the governor. But there is credible eyewitness testimony that Jesse's death was faked, and the man actually killed was Charlie Bigelow, one of Jesse's gang members who had fallen out of favor with him. Bigelow resembled Jesse; in fact he often passed himself off as Jesse. The notorious outlaw was seen and identified as being alive ten years after his supposed death by people who knew him well. At that time he was touring the country with a Wild West show giving shooting exhibitions, using the alias Frank Dalton. He may have had an Indian wife.

It was at this time, when Annette was exploring the possibilities of the Gift of the White Light, that her marriage began to fall part. Her attempts to get things back on track failed. She did not disclose the details to me, but you can tell the pain is still there if you mention it to her.

Annette tried to hide her pain from her friends and children. One day, June, seeing Annette was in the dumps, suggested that they take a yoga class. Annette protested: She was busy with teaching at Dr. Jampolsky's center, doing private consultations, and taking care of the house and the kids. It was a pretty heavy load; she really didn't have time to take a yoga class.

In addition, Annette had not been feeling well: her hips and back were bothering her. She knew the pain was stress-related. June said that was all the more reason to do some yoga—to get rid of the damn stress. This made sense. Okay, Annette said, she'd try to squeeze in the time. Yoga had always helped her relax, so what the hey. Off they went to the class at the Novato Recreation Center.

The young woman who was running the class was a delight, Annette thought, and soon both Annette and June were really into it. Annette felt her bones creaking and jolts of pain as they went through the various postures and positions and stretching, but she could tell the tension was leaving her body.

Then the instructor had everyone in the class lie down on the soft, deep-pile, green carpet for meditation. Annette remembers relaxing easily. She was sinking into a trance, feeling the power of the White Light shining on her, sending her deeper and deeper into the trance state.

An image began to appear: At first it looked like two boxes on a pole; then it became clearer and clearer. Strange—it was a street sign, but she could not make out the names of the streets.

Gradually the signs faded and another image began to form—indistinct at first, like a mist—and Annette thought for a moment she might be seeing another ghost. Soon it was clear: It was definitely a human form, but it wasn't moving. It was horizontal, lying on what looked like a huge shelf suspended in midair. The shape formed into a woman. She had clothes on, but looked bloodless, and Annette knew this was definitely a corpse!

Annette snapped out of her trance and shot straight up, trembling all over.

June, who was lying next to her, asked her if she was all right. Annette shook it off and said she was fine; maybe she was coming down with something.

Annette lay back down and quieted her breathing. What did this vision mean? She had no idea. She was sure of one thing: She did not know the dead woman; she'd never seen her before.

The class was soon over and Annette and June went to their car. Annette told June what she had seen. June was excited. "Wow, seeing dead people you don't even know! You have to go to the police!" June exclaimed.

Annette shook her head. "No way, I can't go to the police! They're going to think I'm crazy! What if a reporter got wind of it? They'd think I'm a nut case. My husband has a responsible job. What if word got out he was married to a crazy person?"

"But listen, Annette, you know your whole life is about helping people. Well, that woman has a mother and a father, maybe a husband and children, and you know you've been shown this vision for a reason."

Annette found a phone booth and called Dick. Even though they were having a rough time in their marriage, she still trusted his judgment. He had great faith in her gift; he said if there was any way she could help the police, she should do it.

Okay, she would go. She came out of the phone booth and asked June if she would mind driving; her knees were knocking too much.

On the way down to the Marin County Sheriff's Office, Annette thought this action was going to change her life. She was either going to help the police and her future course would take a giant turn, or she was going to get herself laughed out of town. Either way, things would not ever be the same.

Annette's First Case

When Annette got off the elevator in the Marin Civic Center—the famous building with the blue roof designed by Frank Lloyd Wright—and saw the large glass doors marked "Marin County Sheriff" she was shaking all over. She hated to be ridiculed, and here she was, leaving herself wide open. What if they just thought of her as a delusional, whacked-out housewife with nothing better to do than waste their time?

June took hold of her arm to steady her as they marched in. Annette sucked in a deep breath and stiffened her spine.

A deputy at the desk, a young man, asked how he might help her.

"I'm here about a murder," Annette said firmly.

"Oh?" He sat up straight.

She looked him in the eye. "I am a psychic and I think I have some information about a dead body."

The young officer cracked a tiny smile. At least she thought he did. "Could you wait a moment? I'll get the detective in charge of…psychics."

Annette glanced at June. They weren't going to take her seriously. June held on to her arm tightly and smiled reassuringly.

The officer returned with a detective. He was a big man in a dark blue suit and he looked all business, like he could take on any number of bad guys.

"Please, ladies," he said. "Follow me."

He opened the half door next to the counter and the two women followed him down a long hallway to a small, windowless room with only a wooden desk and three straight-backed chairs.

The women were asked to have a seat and wait a few minutes. Annette had never been in a police station in her life. And, except for the street confrontation in Mexico with the officer wanting a bribe, she had never really even talked to a policeman more than maybe to say, "Hi." As she sat there, Annette's throat closed up. "June, this sure feels like an interrogation room," Annette said. She'd have given a hundred dollars for a drink of water. Five hundred to be home in bed. Her dang knees wouldn't stop shaking.

A few minutes later two detectives came in. One was of medium height, with thick, black, wavy hair, and an easy smile. He was a natty dresser, pressed out in a rose-colored sport jacket. He shook Annette's hand, introduced himself as Detective Richard Keaton, and introduced the other man as Detective Ken Irving. Irving was taller, slight, quiet, and had very black eyes. He nodded toward Annette and leaned back against the wall. Keaton said later that Ken Irving was a total skeptic at that time, but he was polite to Annette and June.

"How can we help you?" Keaton asked.

"I'm Annette Martin. I'm a professional psychic," Annette said, speaking right up. "I know you're going to think this is crazy, but I had a vision of a body."

She was half hoping he'd simply thank her, give her his card, and say ta-ta.

Instead, without blinking an eye, he said, "I don't think you're crazy. Tell me what you experienced. We have had a murder recently. Do you mind if we record this?"

Annette nodded. "That's fine."

He had a calm, even tone, and Annette perceived that he was a good listener and could see she was nervous. She guessed, too, that he was trying to show he was receptive. She sensed he was a kind man—not at all what she would expect from a policeman—and she felt that his support was coming from his inner being, very deep.

He would say later that he wasn't really into psychic stuff, but as there were no leads, he thought, what the hell, other police agencies had used psychics, sometimes successfully, why not give it a shot? They had a suspect, but he was on the run, and they had no idea where he'd gone.

As June started scribbling notes, Annette told the two detectives about what she'd seen in her vision: the body suspended in midair, how it looked, and the street sign. Their eyes had gotten big when she told them what the victim looked like.

"If I gave you something to hold, would that help?" Keaton asked.

"It might," she said. Good, she thought, he knew about psychometry.

"We'll be right back," Keaton said. The two detectives left and came back in a few minutes. Keaton handed Annette a piece of clothing.

Already Annette was getting goose bumps—an indication that her accuracy would be extremely high—in the 85 to 90 percent range or better.

She closed her eyes and went into a trance, her palms perspiring profusely. A moment later Annette began to describe how the killer had picked up his victim on the street and coaxed her into his car, and how the victim, after he had killed her, had been moved to a metal shed next to a trailer (a mobile home, actually). She described the victim's horribly battered condition.

Keaton was astonished—Annette was giving them details that nobody but the police knew. Before he heard any more, he thought he'd best get some direction from on high. He excused himself and went to his boss's office. His boss was a grizzled homicide detective who had earned his stripes on the mean streets of Oakland, a hard-nosed, go-by-the-book sort.

Keaton told him this psychic was saying things that were right on the money, things that had not been revealed to the media, things she couldn't possibly know unless she'd taken a peek into their files. He asked his boss to come and listen to her. His boss said he didn't have time at the moment, but if she could come back later, he'd love to hear what she had to say.

"No joke?" Keaton asked, astonished.

"Tell her seven, if that's okay?"

"Okay."

He went back to Annette and asked her if she could come back later; the boss wanted to hear what she had to say. "How about seven this evening?"

"All right, I'll come back at seven. Is it okay to bring my husband?"

"Bring anyone you like. My boss and a few others want to ask you some questions."

"Fine," Annette said. "How am I doing? Is any of this right?"

"We'd like to hear more," he said.

On the way out, Annette whispered to June: "Wheh! That was something, huh?"

"I just hope they believe you," June said.

Annette Gets Grilled by the Inquisition

When Annette returned that night, she found the Civic Center different. There was not the hubbub of people that had been there earlier; now the cavernous silence of the inside of the place made her edgy. She was so glad Dick had agreed to come. Even though things between them were not good, she was hoping that if he became involved in her work it might help get their marriage back on track.

Annette, Dick, and June were led by Detective Keaton into a large conference room where fifteen to twenty people were waiting: more detectives, the Marin County sheriff, the captain of the detectives, lieutenants, the district attorney and some of his staff, and a couple of FBI agents. Annette felt a bit overwhelmed. To her, they all looked formal and grim. They were seated in a semicircle, with Keaton, whom Annette felt had the only really friendly face in the room, seated opposite her. This was like facing a tryout for an opera, or Dr. Jampolsky's panel of skeptical doctors—only a hundred times worse. Annette was a trained singer and an experienced medical intuitive, but this…this was cops and killers, this was totally different. She wasn't ready for this.

Dick gave her hand a reassuring squeeze. June smiled her encouragement and got out her notebook.

The following account of the interview with the Marin County sheriffs is taken directly from June Rucker's notes. For legal reasons, some of the names and places have been changed, but otherwise this is a true and accurate account, edited only for the sake of brevity.

Introductions were made; coffee was served. To Annette it felt like a trial, and she was being judged. Her stomach was in knots.

Before she began, Detective Keaton asked her if she'd like to explain how she goes about doing a reading, which was exactly what she had been thinking she ought to do.

She explained that when she did a reading on the phone she always asked for an original photo, which has an invisible energy field that is left on it, just like a fingerprint. She explained her mind could read the signals coming from that energy field like a radio picking up signals from the atmosphere.

Detective Keaton asked her if she could read clothing and other things as well.

Annette said she could. "Whatever we touch we leave an invisible print on, whether it's a dress, shoes, jewelry, furniture, anything. When I enter into a state of complete relaxation I take three deep breaths, all the while visualizing white light coming in through my frontal lobe and circulating through my body. My conscious mind slows down and my subconscious mind takes over."

She scanned the room and saw some encouraging faces, and a whole bunch of skeptics.

"Okay," Detective Keaton said, "Is it all right if we record this session?"

"Yes," she said. An audio tape recorder was turned on.

Detective Keaton asked Annette if she'd like to see some of the victim's clothing. She said she would. They gave her a piece of clothing that she clutched in her hands. She took three deep breaths and slipped into a trance. She was perspiring.

After a few moments, Annette said, "I see a black car…he killed her and wrapped her in a tarp…

June noted the group seemed to tense at this; some of them glanced at each other. She had it right; for sure she had it right.

Annette continued: "He wrapped her in a tarp or a blanket of some kind and put her outside the door of a trailer…".Annette paused again, seeming to nod as if what she were about to say was important. "It's like he has two definite personalities. Crazy.Will kill again. Hit her on the right eye, a lethal blow—went north and northeast into Nevada. Stopped along the way in sawmill country. Nevada plates on the car— can't see the numbers. Yes, Jekyll-Hyde personality. Hot where he is now.Very dry, [the victim had on] blue shirt."

She paused again, sweat streaming down her face, then resumed a moment later:"He picked up the girl at a corner of some street near her work. No struggle. The girl excited at first…fear? Sexual excitement?"

She swallowed, paused. Her voice was cracking. She was seeing a scene in her mind's eye worse than any horror film.

"Other people involved…two men helping him. One very thin— two girls! Took black car on a dirt road—like a meeting place. Group of people. He called some buddies from a phone at a phone booth, a wooden phone booth—they went out on this road, buddies giving him advice to put the car somewhere…"

She shook her head. June realized that the time line was all jumbled up, Annette was getting random images, but the hairs on her arms—the goose bumps—were continually standing up during the whole session.

When Annette stopped shaking, June took her pulse and told her she needed to calm herself. Detective Irving got her a glass of orange juice.

Annette resumed a few moments later: "The murderer threw up after he killed her…went to pieces when he'd found out what he'd done [in his other personality]. He'd gone into a rage over some stupid thing and lost complete control of himself…she screamed when he came at her."

Detective Keaton asked why didn't anyone hear her scream.

Annette paused for a few moments, then said, "It happened at two in the afternoon; there was no one around. I see him burying some- thing—he's very excited—around the other side of the trailer, he's dig- ging—very shallow. He's shaking like a leaf. He went out and got a tarp and wrapped her up. Couple of stairs on the trailer, bumped her on one—took her around the other side and buried her. Shallow. Then he changes his mind and digs her up and puts her in the shed that is next to the trailer and locks the door."

Annette gasped, and went on: "He's going crazy. His wife's going to come home soon. All the blood everywhere, he's in a panic over what to do.

"Ah! He calls somebody—his knees are giving out, he's falling apart. He can hardly breathe, almost commits suicide—in the personality that feels guilt—he's sweating, about to throw up. Pay phone not far, he walked—so shaky—he almost messed his pants."

Annette took a deep breath. "He calls somebody, his buddy. He changes clothes—khaki, beige, gold watchband, there's a crude tattoo on his arm, the initials 'R.T.' and a blue-green anchor. He's really crazy now. He takes a drug or something to calm himself and calls San Francisco. Calls Nola…sounds like, a name. He now wraps the bloody clothes and buries them with the body…

At one point, Dick could not listen to any more; he looked like he might faint or throw up. He left the room. Later he'd tell Annette that he was astounded at how far her psychic abilities had progressed, but it was too gruesome for him.

June reported that Annette looked exhausted now.

Detective Keaton said: "Can you describe him?"

Annette paused, then said: "He has short hair, high forehead, a good-looking man with a few lines across the forehead, curly hair, kind of light, olive skin. Open short sleeve shirt. He worries. Oh, God! He has to stay calm….The end of the trailer is facing west, the sun hitting the top of the trailer. He's calmed down now, drugged. Methadone. Cocky. Thinks he's fooled you. Gambling at Harrah's Tahoe. Greyhound bus going through Tahoe, stopped there. Gas station, stopped in Reno, no gambling. He's in Elko, Nevada now, Highway 40…"

The images were coming in a flurry. The gist of it was, he picked up a black car with blue-and-white license plates in Nevada from a blond woman. He drove alone through the desert. He had money. He was heading for Salt Lake, where he planned to drop off the car and take another Greyhound bus. He was carrying a brown-and-yellow suitcase tied with a piece of yellow rope, although there were not many clothes in it.

Detective Keaton asked Annette if she'd draw a sketch of the killer, which she did. She added that he had a low, rough voice. He had asthma, which caused difficulty breathing in the upper chest…

That evening session lasted almost five hours. At one point Detective Keaton asked Annette if she could get any vibrations off a set of keys, and she took them in her hand and goose bumps appeared all over her face. A moment later, she flung them across the room. They were the killer's keys: They caused her to get into his head and feel the thrill he felt at the time of the murder, to see it all over again in her mind's eye.

But Annette took the keys again. There were six keys. She correctly identified five of them easily: his car, the trailer, and so on. She held up the last key and announced that it belonged to a locker or a box of some kind and it made her feel sad and angry when she touched it.

Tears started down her face.

"This key leads to where the body is!" she said.

"Amazing," Detective Keaton said. "Absolutely correct! That key goes to the locker where we found the body. You are absolutely amazing!" he exclaimed.

She continued her reading.

She told them that they would catch him wearing white—on his job at an institution (turned out to be in a nursing home). She said he would be found outside of California and elude them for a year—which turned out to be exactly correct almost to the day.

The next day Annette went with Detective Keaton and his boss to the mobile home park where the crime had been committed. Beads of perspiration broke out on her palms immediately. She had no trouble picking out the killer's mobile home and the metal shed where he'd kept the body of his victim. Years later in an episode of "48 Hours" on TV, Annette returned to this very place and again had no trouble picking out the exact spot. She said the vibrations had not dimmed, despite the years.

She directed the police to a bar in Novato where the suspect had used the phone booth—an old-fashioned, wooden phone booth which she had described perfectly. Phone company records showed a call to a relative of the killer at the time the killer would have been there.

She told the officers that the killer would kill again and again until they stopped him. As it turned out, the suspect did try to kill again. He slashed the throat of a young woman in Washington state, covered her with dirt and leaves, and stood by to watch her die, but somebody came along and he ran. The victim lived.

Detective Keaton had been won over completely. But he was already realizing that though Annette was giving them great information, the trick was using it to bag the killer without jeopardizing the DA's case. Also, sometimes she gave incomplete flashes that weren't too useful. He would have to learn to ask her the right questions. Over the years he would hone that skill.

Annette realized that this ability she had to get into the mind of a vicious criminal was a great tool. It made her feel ill to read the killer's thoughts and see the horrible thing he'd done to that woman—but that didn't matter. If she could help get homicidal maniacs off the street, she was willing to suffer.

The killer in this case was arrested in Washington state and convicted of the other crime that Annette had predicted. He is now incarcerated there and probably will die in prison. At this time there are no plans to bring him back to California to face charges.

Chapter Nine

Annette's Career as a Psychic Detective

Annette Martin…Without any doubt, is a crucial element in the fight against crime in its worst form. Because of her dedication, belief, temperance, and fortitude against evil, she is well admired and respected as a proven loyal professional by members of law enforcement.
—D. J. Miller, retired San Francisco supervisor and former magistrate judge

Since her first case, Annette has worked on over forty others. There is not space enough in this book to recount them all, so I have selected a representative group. In some, her work has resulted in an arrest and conviction; in others, the police failed to follow up on the clues she'd given them; in still others, there wasn't enough evidence to prove guilt. Annette's visions, of course, have no legal standing.

Some of Annette's cases involve the most brutal and heinous crimes one could imagine. Others involve finding missing persons where no crime has been committed.

Annette and the Lost Young Man

On a warm June afternoon, the parents of twenty-one-year-old Phil Cullen came bursting into Annette's office desperate for her to do a reading. They had heard about Annette through friends in the neighborhood. Annette was on a break between clients and agreed to see them. Mr. and Mrs. Cullen were frantic. Their son was mentally ill: He suffered from multiple personality disorder and was often delusional. He had gone on a trip to Florida with his older cousin and had wandered off in Miami and neither the cousin nor the Miami police could find him. Not a trace. It had been almost a week.

The parents had brought along a photo of the young man taken at a birthday party. He was nice-looking, blond, with bright, blue eyes gazing at the camera happily.

Annette sat down, closed her eyes, took in her three deep breaths, and began the reading.

She said that their son definitely had two personalities: one, calm and rational; the other, highly emotional, easily angered, and prone to rages. And he was extremely irrational. She said that having two personalities was making him feel up and down, as if he were on a seesaw. She scribbled lines on her yellow tablet that went all over the place and she fell deeper into her trance. "He has times when he could be violent," she said, "and hurt himself or others. He has to stay on his medications."

"Yes," the boy's mother said. "Phil has been diagnosed as schizophrenic by doctors. It's a constant problem. The medications make him ill, so he stops taking them."

"Without the medications he goes into deep depressions and becomes more delusional," Annette said.

"Yes," his mother said. "We are so worried about what he might do to himself or others."

"I see he was in a place with bars—a hospital—and that the treatment didn't work."

"No, it didn't," his mother said. "That was in Alaska."

Annette saw flashes of Phil walking down a busy street in a big city. He didn't seem to know where he was or how he got there. "He feels this emotional personality has taken over and he feels lost within himself," she said. Annette slid deeper into her trance. Then she said she saw tall buildings with enormous windows...and she was getting her goose bumps, meaning she was almost certainly correct. "Yes, he's in New York. I'm quite sure. He feels cold...he looks gaunt as if he's not getting enough to eat. I see a jacket on his arm, but he hasn't got a suitcase."

Phil's father said, "That's right, he didn't have a suitcase!"

Annette said, "He's wearing a crude medal around his neck. A cross."

"He made that when he was in the hospital," Phil's father said. "He was so proud of it."

His mother asked how in the world did he get to New York?

Annette let the images flash through her mind. "He got on a bus without a ticket and the driver could see he was disturbed and felt sorry for him, so he let him stay on the bus."

Phil's parents looked at each other. Annette knew what they were thinking: New York, such a large city—how were they ever going to find him?

Annette went back into her trance. She saw him continue down the street in a daze, and then Annette gasped. She saw a group of young men coming towards him; they were dressed in saffron robes—Hare Krishnas!

They approached him and talked to him, and Phil went with them.

"But where in New York are they?" Mrs. Cullen asked.

Annette focused in on a street sign, a numbered street on the east side in mid-Manhattan. And then she said she saw an Irish policeman who wants to go looking for Phil.

"That would be my husband's nephew, John Cullen," Phil's mother said. "He has offered to help."

"I see a street sign. Tell him to go to the east side of Manhattan in the fifties. The houses have stairs going up, not far from where the young Hare Krishnas found him. Your son is in a house with a big living room, and with something like a bay window looking out on the street. It's two stories; the kitchen is in back. You walk through a hallway, you come in, and there is this arch…"

"Do you see numbers on the house?"

Annette rarely saw numbers. But this time she gave them an address, and even though it was hazy, it was the exact address. "There's a grocery store right nearby. Phil is quite sickly now, and a girl with long, brown hair is taking him to a hospital, 'Saint' something…I can't make out the name…Do not worry, he'll be fine and will be home with you soon."

Off-duty Palo Alto detective John Cullen did go to New York, and after some initial confusion, followed Annette's instructions and found Phil staying with the Hare Krishnas. The address Annette had given was exactly correct and there was a grocery store nearby just as she had said.

But since he was staying with them of his own volition and he was of legal age, the Hare Krishnas refused to make him leave. There was nothing the police or Detective John Cullen could do.

The parents knew the trouble Phil could get into if he were off his medications and they came once again to Annette for help.

She told them to go to the Hare Krishna headquarters in San Francisco and give them Phil's medical history…"They wouldn't want to be responsible for anything if he should become violent."

They did, and Annette was right, the Hare Krishnas didn't want to be responsible. A little more than a week later, the Cullens went to New York and picked up their son. He later got on the right medications and his condition greatly improved.

More Missing Persons Cases

Not all of Annette's cases had a happy outcome for the subject, unfortunately. Take the case of seventy-four-year-old Ralph Thomas, who disappeared on a sunny Saturday in late September 1991. The subject said good-bye to his wife, went out walking early in the morning in San Francisco, and never came back. The police had no clue. Annette was brought into the case after he'd been missing a couple of weeks.

A detective, Mark North, from the Marin County Sheriff's Office brought Annette a photograph of the missing man, gave her his age and place of residence, and the date of his disappearance. That's all she had to go on.

Annette sat back, pressed the photo between her palms, and went into her trance. Soon she was feeling goose bumps. This time she was to be astonishingly accurate.

The first thing Annette said was that Thomas had an irregular heart beat. She saw a small scar on his nose. She said that there was a Scottish plaid hat in his room, but that he was wearing a beige hat when he went missing. He went for a walk by the ocean in San Francisco at dawn. He loved walking, feeling the warmth of the sun on his face, breathing the sea air.

Then, Annette said, "He took a bus and crossed the Golden Gate Bridge and went to Fairfax (a town in Marin County, north of San Francisco). He got off the bus and crossed the street and went into a coffee shop." She described the coffee shop as white with latticework, and reported that Thomas was looking at a map or something, a bus schedule perhaps, as he was drinking coffee. She also noted he was suffering from hypoglycemia.

"He left the coffee shop and took a bus with the numbers 2 and 3, going to the town of Bolinas." She saw him getting off the bus and hiking into a wooded area. He wanted to be alone. She said he carried no wallet and he had something shiny on his jacket. He was wearing short pants, long socks, hiking boots, a jacket, and the beige hat. She said as he walked he was "bound up," as if he had prostrate problems.

Then on her yellow tablet Annette drew a map of the area. The road he was on branched up and down; he took the lower road. He crossed a stream, then walked down a road where there was a ravine, she said, a sharp slope with a lot of rocks. She said she saw him in pain, doubled over, maybe trying to pass a stone, and he fell down into the ravine.

"I smell death!" she cried suddenly, then added: "I see a hat! You will find his body in a small ravine with a great many rocks. His left hand will be sticking up from the rocks. His beige hat was still on his head."

When the detective went to the subject's home, he found the plaid hat—just as Annette had described it—and his wallet.

The man's grandson said he had a shiny button on his jacket.

Using dogs, the police searched the area Annette had mapped out and discovered the body lying in exactly the place Annette had described. Thomas had taken bus number 23 to get to this trail. His left hand was the only thing visible, just as she said, sticking up from the rocks, and the beige hat was still on his head.

The man had died of either accidental or natural causes.

Annette Has the Flu

Annette had a similar case in San Rafael, another town in Marin County, a year later. On December 10, 1992, Annette was sick in bed with the flu and a temperature of 102 when she was contacted to see what she could do in the case of Joseph Prior, who was missing from a nursing home. It seems the elderly Mr. Prior had wandered off during the night and, so far, the man's family, the nursing home staff, and the police could not find a trace of him. There were heavy rainstorms in the area at the time and the family were worried there might be a tragedy if he were not found soon.

Annette said if they'd send a photo of the man by messenger she'd see what she could do. As she put the phone down, she lay back in her sick bed, and before she drifted off to sleep she had a spontaneous and powerful vision. She found herself in a park and caught a glimpse of a dark complected man walking in what she felt certain was an easterly direction toward a bridge over a creek swollen with the rains. She saw the man fall into the water head first directly under the bridge. Annette felt the coldness of death close over him.

Then she must have drifted off to sleep, because the next thing she knew her doorbell was ringing. The photo had arrived.

After the courier left, Annette sat down, put herself in the usual trance, and immediately saw the same scene she'd envisioned earlier: the same bridge, the same creek, and the same man, dead!

A few days later the police called to say that they had not found the man. The place Annette had described was in a park where the man often walked, but a thorough search had not turned up anything. She suggested that he was still there; they should keep looking.

Detective Keaton called a few weeks later, and as soon as she said hello, he shouted; "You did it again, Annette! Some girls playing in the area discovered Mr. Joseph Prior. His body was in the creek right under the bridge, just like you described!"

It seems the creek, during the rains, had turned into a torrent, and when the water subsided, there was the body.

Annette never did get a "thank you" from the rest home. Perhaps they thought she might castigate them for not supervising their patient more rigorously.

The Green Man

Another missing person case occurred on May 1, 1997. This case was subsequently featured on a "Psychic Detectives" episode on Court TV in May of 2005 and replayed on NBC the following June.

Dennis Prado had gone hiking early in the morning. No one was sure where he had gone, but he often walked in a large park on the San Francisco peninsula near Pacifica. He had never returned from this particular hike. Detective Fernando Realyvasques of the Pacifica Police Department headed up the investigation for two months. Police and search-and-rescue personnel searched the entire park several times and found not a trace of the man. The man's family pressured Detective Realyvasques to bring Annette in on the case. He reported, "I had to get permission from my supervisors because [working with psychics] is not something we normally do."

In her trance, Annette saw the color green everywhere. And then she saw Mr. Prado hiking in the park, veering off the main path, and turning onto a dirt path toward a hill. She thought he went up the hill to take in the scenery—there's a view of the Pacific Ocean and the beaches—and maybe take a rest. She saw him clutch his chest and felt his pain, then saw him stagger into the underbrush, collapse, and die. She said that there had been no foul play, that it was a natural death. She added that a person would not find him; he would be found by a dog.

Detective Realyvasques asked Annette to indicate on a map where the body might be found. She traced the route she felt Mr. Prado had taken and drew a small circle on the map where she felt a "warm spot." She said he'd be found in the center of the circle.

She was pretty certain she was right: She was covered head to toe with goose bumps.

The detective said the area had been searched and sniffed by dogs—twice.

Annette rolled her eyes. "Nevertheless," she said, "that's where you will find the man's body."

A team of search-and-rescue volunteers went back to the area and in twenty-five minutes one of their dogs found the body in the center of the small (less than one-eighth of a mile in diameter) circle Annette had drawn on the map!

What does Detective Realyvasques think of psychics now? "If we didn't have [Annette's] information, because he was all dressed in green, covered with brush, and embedded with dirt we wouldn't have found him. Do I believe [in Annette's powers]? I don't have a choice. That's the honest answer."

The Case of the Missing Priest

In some cases, as I mentioned earlier, Annette's insights are tragically ignored by the police.

One such case that occurred during the summer of 1982 in Santa Fe, New Mexico, involved a missing person, Father Reynaldo Rivera, a popular Franciscan priest at Saint Francis Cathedral.

Father Rivera received a call one evening from a man who stated that his sister was dying and wanted last rites. The caller gave what later proved to be a false name. The priest agreed to meet with the man, who said he would take him to his sister.

Father Rivera was last seen leaving the rectory about 7 P.M. in his tan Chevy Malibu. He was to meet the man at a freeway rest stop thirteen miles south of Santa Fe on Interstate 25 near a couple of phone booths. Another priest had overheard the conversation on the phone, so this much was known.

When Father Rivera failed to return to the rectory, a missing person's case was assigned to detectives with the New Mexico state police. Detective Dennis J. Miller, who later sent Annette a comprehensive report of this case, was a Santa Fe city detective assigned to assist the state police.

The initial investigation didn't turn up a clue. The public was in an uproar. Father Rivera was a well-liked priest from a very large parish. A fellow detective recommended that Detective Miller contact Annette.

Detective Miller remembers that when he called her she told him she had a tremendous workload, but she was "kind, professional, caring, and concerned." Detective Miller sent Annette a photo of the priest, his name and date of birth, and the date and place of his disappearance. At that time they knew nothing else. The material was sent through Detective Keaton at the Marin County Sheriff's Office.

Before Annette did her reading there was a break in the case. The priest's car was found at a rest stop on Interstate 25, but not the one the priest was supposed to have gone to. This rest stop was near Grants, New Mexico, 120 miles from Santa Fe.

The car was found locked, with the windows rolled up. When the crime lab team went over the scene they were amazed to find that there were no fingerprints on the vehicle whatsoever, and no hair, lint, threads, or any other kind of foreign matter. And, the gas tank was completely dry. The police were stumped.

On the seventh day following the disappearance, Father Rivera's body was found by some kids in an open field just off the dirt road leading to the tiny town of Waldo, New Mexico, a road used mostly by hunters.

Detective Miller describes the scene:

> *Father Rivera's body was resting on its back. His arms were extended out to either side and his legs were slightly apart. He had on a black shirt, black trousers secured with a black leather belt, and black shoes. His eyes were opened and had such a horrid and terrifying look as though he had seen the devil himself. His eyes appeared to be greenish-gray with tear-*

*streak stains running from both corners downward. The three-strand barbed
wire used to strangle him was still wrapped around his mouth and head
several times, and it was stretched so tight that the barb wire was imbedded
into his facial skin. His chest, the black shirt, had the imprint of a right
shoe print as though he had been stomped on also. His shirt was partially
open to reveal the chest area; slice marks from a sharp object had been
made in (an X) and crisscross pattern…*

No one had been seen nearby. A recent rain had obliterated any
footprints in the surrounding area.

Several days passed. Despite a great effort by state and local police,
there were still no leads or solid clues as to who the perpetrators were or
where they had gone. Father Rivera's turquoise money clip had been
taken and officers were checking all the pawnshops in New Mexico. So
far, no hits. Meanwhile, Father Rivera was honored by the biggest funeral
in New Mexico history. The public was demanding action.

Detective Miller had not heard from Annette. When he called her she
said she'd sent the tape of her trance session back to him two weeks earlier
through the Marin County Sheriff's Office. When he checked, he discovered that the package had been mislaid. When Detective Miller finally
received the tape of Annette's reading a few days later, he was dumbfounded.
The tape contained the following observations, which Detective Miller
already knew:

— that the priest had been called away under false pretenses
— that he was lured to a place with parked cars and picnic tables
   (the rest stop)
— that the suspect had requested to meet him near phone booths
   (at the rest stop)
— that there was a green sign with a "W" on it with the small letter
   "a" (the Waldo exit)
— that the victim had been assaulted and his hands were tied behind
   him with barbed wire
— that his face and head were bound with barbed wire
— that his chest had been slashed in an "X" pattern (Annette added
   that the knife was long and had a pearl handle, facts which
   Detective Miller was not aware of.)

— that the death was so horrifying that Father Rivera died with his eyes open and slightly squinted, "as if he'd seen hell."

Annette gave other details of which the police had no knowledge, including a description and crude sketches of two suspects and a blow-by-blow horrific account of how the priest died. She described one of the killers as a Mexican national. She said he was deformed and walked with a limp and his body was slightly twisted when he stood and walked. He was dark-complected and had almost shoulder-length, brown hair. She said he lived or worked at or near a place called "The Pink Poodle."

Detective Miller said that all of what Annette reported was, as far as he knew, true. And, in Santa Fe, there was a restaurant/hotel called "The Pink Poodle."

Miller was astonished by Annette's accuracy and he was very excited about the new clues concerning the suspects. He wrote the following in his account of the incident:

> *Ms. Martin was never given any details of the case nor the condition of the body as it was found or even where it was discovered. Yet, her taped statement, sketches, and description of the area, condition of the body, and identification of the items believed to have been used in the murder are as accurate as can be, all the way to the last detail.*

Given this, you'd suspect the cops might hightail it down to "The Pink Poodle" and see if the Mexican national she described might have worked there, or hung out there...

But no.

Detective Miller could not investigate: It was not his case. The state cops were in charge of this one. What did the state cops do with the information Annette had provided?

Nothing. Absolutely nothing.

Apparently the state cops did not believe in using psychics, even though they had no other leads. Eventually the public fervor died down. As Detective Miller says, "The case just faded away."

No arrests were ever made.

The Polly Klass Case

Petaluma is a small, suburban city north of San Francisco, a quiet, friendly sort of place often mentioned in the "Peanuts" cartoon strip as the birthplace of Charlie Brown's dog, Snoopy. There, on the night of October 1, 1993, twelve-year-old Polly Klass was having her first-ever slumber party with two of her friends. They were having a great time playing silly games. When Polly went to another room she was confronted by a hulking intruder armed with a knife. Polly, in order to protect her friends and family, did not scream. She was overheard telling the man who was taking her away, "Please don't hurt my mom."

Lieutenant Mark North of the Marin County Sheriff's Office, who had worked with Annette before, called her the next morning at eight. His daughter, one of Polly's close friends, had been invited to the slumber party, but had cancelled at the last minute.

In her reading, done without a photograph, Annette saw a knife and a man of about forty, with a beard and a round face. She saw that Polly's abductor had been watching her and that he had brought something to tie up the girls. She saw the name "Richard" and an "R" and a "J." The man who subsequently confessed to the crime was Richard Allen Davis, thirty-nine. Later, the woman who called the cops turned out to be Naomi Jaffe. Davis's car was stuck in the mud on her property.

Annette had reported that the man who committed this vile act was a con man, and he had had a lot of trouble with the law, mostly involving women. This proved true: Davis was a con man and had abused women. Annette saw the number 2 and the number 5—meaning miles. She told Lieutenant North she saw a river and a bridge that looked like an erector set, and she saw Polly's body in a culvert or gully, with wooden boards over her. The girl was already dead.

Meanwhile, thousands of local residents went to work trying to find Polly, during what was soon to become the largest manhunt in human history. Two billion pictures of Polly were passed out. Hundreds of volunteers worked night and day for sixty-five days to find her.

When they finally found Polly's body, Annette had been right on the money with all the information she had reported in her reading. Polly's body was twenty-five miles from where she was taken on November 28, in a gully covered with discarded pieces of wood. Davis, who was sporting a beard, was caught and he confessed to the crime on December 4.

Lieutenant North had tried to get the police and the FBI, who had been brought into the case, to look for Polly's body based on the information Annette had provided, but they dismissed her input as irrelevant.

Even if they had listened to Annette, they would not have been able to save Polly's life, but they might have found her body sooner.

The Edda Kane Case

Another brutal murder was that of Edda Kane, one more case where Annette described the killer with amazing accuracy.

August 20, 1979, was a golden, warm, beautiful day on Mount Tamalpais, a 2,571-foot peak in a state park in Marin County, less than twenty miles north of San Francisco. "Mount Tam," as the locals call it, is thickly covered with native shrubs and grasses, Douglas fir, oaks, and redwoods, with a few rocky cliffs poking out here and there. Wildlife abounds: squirrels, deer, wild boar, foxes. Hawks gently circle in the sky. To the southeast, the graceful, massive chunk of red steel, the Golden Gate Bridge, gleams in the sun, and, beyond, the hills of San Francisco.

From the western slope of Mount Tam you can see the Pacific Ocean, shimmering blue as far as the eye can see. Mount Tam is a wonderful place to hike. It is crisscrossed with well-worn, narrow, dirt trails and little clearings and meadows—great for lazing or picnicking.

Edda Kane, age forty-four, loved to hike there—alone. She enjoyed the solitude, feeling at one with nature and God, walking along the western slope of the mountain on Rock Springs Trail on the way to the quaint West Point Inn.

At about noon, two hikers found her naked, battered body, with a bullet wound in her head. The medical examiner determined that she'd been raped, sodomized, then shot "execution style" while she was on her knees. Begging for her life, perhaps.

The police quickly ruled out the usual suspects: friends, coworkers, neighbors, and relatives. They all had solid alibis and, as far as the police could tell, none of them fit the profile of a psychopathic rapist and killer. The investigators were pretty sure Ms. Kane was raped and killed by a complete stranger, but they had no clue as to who this stranger might be. The only solid evidence they had was the bullet, and they had no match for it.

Annette was called in.

She went out to the scene of the crime with Detective Richard Keaton. It was a hot day, well into the nineties.

When they got out of the car, before they were anywhere near the crime scene, Annette said, "I believe that the suspect was watching the victim from a distance, possibly with the use of binoculars attached to a frayed leather strap."

Keaton took a note. This was amazing even to him; Annette wasn't in her trance yet. He could see she was perspiring, and it was obvious from the sweat on her forehead and goose flesh on her arms that she was starting to get her vibes.

They began walking the trail. Keaton noted that Annette continued to look up the slope of the mountain and seemed interested in the radar station higher up. He knew where the body had been found, but he continued to walk past the site, wondering if Annette would notice. He admitted later that he was secretly testing her.

They continued walking on the path about a quarter of a mile. Keaton noticed Annette had slowed down; her breathing had become heavy. She said she felt warm and hot. As they passed the crime scene, Annette said she had a strong feeling of fear.

Annette looked around the area and said she believed the killer first spotted the victim when he was on a trail higher up. They moved up the hill.

They came to an intersection of the Rock Springs Trail with another, even narrower, trail that wound its way upwards. It was steep and rocky and hard to climb. Annette said she wanted to go that way; she was certain the killer had been on that trail.

Keaton suggested they stay on the Rock Springs Trail.

"Why?" Annette said. "We've already passed the place where she was killed!"

Keaton was flabbergasted. He admitted they had. She had passed the test.

Annette showed him that her palms were sweating. "I could tell by the way my body's been reacting."

They turned around and went back. Keaton swears that absolutely no indication was given as to where the murder happened, but Annette turned off the trail and made her way about fifty yards up the hill. Here she started breathing heavily again. She was turning red and her palms were perspiring profusely.

Keaton asked if she was all right.

"I feel frightened. I think I might throw up!" Annette exclaimed.

She realized later that she was feeling what the victim must have felt.

Annette moved on. She located the spot where the victim had been found. She kept breathing deeply and after a few moments seemed to be feeling better.

"This is it, isn't it, Richard?" She meant it was the place where Edda Kane had been killed.

"It is," he admitted.

Annette said she wanted to sit down and concentrate her thoughts on what had occurred. She was but a few feet from where the body had been found.

Keaton handed Annette some of the victim's belongings, her wristwatch and a sock. Annette held them in her hands and went into her trance.

Almost immediately she started shaking and sweating. "She's terrified! She's running! He's after her! She knew she was being watched—woman's intuition! She heard someone shouting at her, but she didn't stop. He caught her—and she knew him!"

This, of course, was contrary to what the police believed. They had pretty much ruled out everyone who knew Edda Kane as suspects.

Annette's voice choked. "Yes, she knew this man…He took her to this clearing at gunpoint and made her undress, but she didn't do it quickly enough, so he started pulling at her clothing, and he tore the shoulder of a blouse or a jacket as the victim was undressing. She removed her own pants, which were khaki or beige [trying to placate him]. The killer removed his pants and undershorts and pushed the crotch area into the victim's face and said: 'This is what you wanted, wasn't it? You wanted it so bad, go ahead and smell it!'"

Annette was sobbing now, feeling the terror and humiliation of the victim. Her face and arms were covered in goose bumps.

"He slapped her again and again," she said. "He made her perform sexual perversions for over an hour."

Annette said the victim kept saying she'd do anything he wanted, just so he wouldn't hurt her. Annette had to steady herself. She came out of her trance and wiped her brow.

Keaton was shaken, too. He asked if they should knock off.

Annette said no. She sat down and went into her trance again, and for the next two hours she recited details of the crime and the killer's life:

> *She (the victim) senses his craziness, but thinks if she cooperates she will not be killed, but she fears he will disfigure her. The perpetrator is saying all kinds of insane, incoherent things as he's doing this, calling her a bitch, a whore, and worse. He mocks her [the victim's] husband and calls him a "silly old man"…He then made her lie down, swearing at her, berating and denigrating her and all women. He said that she had been teasing him and that she had misunderstood his intentions. She tried to say she was sorry, but he scoffed. Then he proceeded to sodomize her. He screamed how he hated women and that she was like the rest of them. She was lying on her stomach now, wearing nothing but her socks. He kept saying that she had teased him and mocked him. He tried again to sodomize her and her rage overcame her terror; she turned and called him a pig, lashing out at him. And that is when he put the gun to her head and shot her.*

"To her," Annette said, "it sounded like a cannon being fired in a tunnel. She felt a severe pain. There's massive bleeding; the victim knows she's dying."

Annette collapsed onto the ground, holding her head. "She's dying," she said. "Blood gushing down over her head and neck. She feels horribly alone, and humiliated, feeling sorry for her husband and how terrible he'll feel when he hears she died in this way, violated, and left naked." Annette added that the victim felt oddly guilty since she knew she had teased her killer on at least two occasions.

Annette said nothing for a long moment. Then she stood up, her hair blowing in the wind. It was as if she had shifted gears. The tears stopped; her features grew grim.

"After he killed her, he was confused and felt panicked. He kicked the body on the legs. He gathered up her clothing, wrapping the gun in the victim's blouse and then in her beige or khaki pants, and put them in a greenish-colored backpack…Wait, there's a weird, pungent odor.

"His thoughts are confused. He doesn't know what to do. He leaves the area, going up and over and down…"

She added that he had not come there intending to kill Ms. Kane, but merely to humiliate her.

Keaton asked Annette to describe the killer's genitals—was he circumcised, and so on—which she did.

He'd taken revenge for the teasing he had received from the victim, Annette said. This teasing had been noted by Annette in a previous reading she'd done at the sheriff's office. The teasing had occurred when the victim had visited the killer at his apartment.

Now Annette described the killer's apartment: a small kitchen with glasses in the sink and a left upper cabinet over the sink with many flavors of tea; a cluttered living room with a hanging lamp attached to the ceiling, a small green lamp on a table, a green couch with a pattern on it, and two chairs. The couch and chairs were piled high with clutter. She saw that he'd hidden the gun he used on Edda Kane in a closet; she described the gun as being dark and large, a revolver. It was located near some colored stones.

When Keaton visited this apartment in the course of his investigation, he found it exactly as Annette had described it. Without any physical evidence to tie the suspect to the crime, however, he could not obtain a warrant and was not able to do a thorough search.

The teasing that the victim recalled with her dying breath involved the messiness of the apartment and some harmless flirtation. Annette said further that she heard Edda Kane's voice saying that she felt the leaves falling down on her body.

When Edda Kane's body was found, it was lying face down with perhaps a dozen leaves on top of her. Keaton had seen this before the body was moved.

Annette went on to talk about the killer, how he had brain damage and a tendency to forget and to black out things that were unpleasant to him. She said the brain damage might be due to drug use or to childhood disease, maybe both.

She said that he loved to come to Mount Tam, that it freed his mind, that he felt entrapped in his mind and his body and often seemed distant, that some people thought he was clairvoyant, but he was not. He did not get along with his parents.

And then she said that he did not get along with his fellow employees at work and that he was a loner, that he frequently spent time out-of-doors to clear his head, and he did a lot of walking. She described the killer as having frequent mood changes.

That day on Mount Tam, Annette tried to find the killer's escape route. She and Keaton drove around on mountain roads and trails. Annette was certain that the killer had parked his car near the local Air Force barracks.

She "saw" him coming out of the park, sweating profusely and very scared, biting his lip. "He's frantic to get rid of her clothes that he has in the backpack," she said. "He drove off toward the Bolinas–Fairfax area..." She wanted to continue, but Keaton thought she looked exhausted and, due to the lateness of the hour, broke it off.

Annette thought the clothing and the gun would never be found. She said the killer was sure that the police would think that "some kooky nut followed her, raped her, and killed her." He seemed certain he would not be suspected.

The conclusion to this case was odd. The man Annette described as the killer was, after her reading, high on the police suspect list. They interviewed his coworkers and neighbors and so on, and perhaps he felt the law closing in on him. Two months after Annette did her reading, the man hanged himself. He did not leave a suicide note, and neither the gun nor Edda Kane's clothing were found, just as Annette has predicted.

David Carpenter, the "Trailside Killer," was stalking and killing women on Mount Tam during the same time and many writers have included Edda Kane as one of his victims, even though the bullet that killed her did not come from either of the two weapons that David Carpenter is known to have used in his crimes. David Carpenter was convicted of murder in two separate trials and sentenced to death in both cases, but the police never made a case that he was Edda Kane's killer and he was never charged.

Twenty years later the Discovery Channel and BBC broadcasted a special based upon a reenactment of this case.

The Edda Kane case remains officially open.

The Buddy Thompson Case

This is the case of a Tennessee man named Buddy Thompson who went missing April 13, 1999. At the time it was discovered he was missing, no one had seen him for several days and there were no clues as to his whereabouts. The recorded sessions presented below were held in Annette's office in Saratoga, California, beginning at 2 P.M. on June 10, 1999. At the request of the family and the police agency involved, the names have been changed. Present at the session were Richard Keaton and Annette.

Keaton had recently retired from the Marin County Sheriff's Office and was working with Annette in the capacity of a private eye. The only information Keaton and Annette had was the man's name and that he was missing. By this time, having worked with Annette for almost twenty years, Keaton was extremely adept at asking Annette the right questions in order to elicit answers which would be most valuable to investigators. The tape begins:

KEATON: We have a wallet and some writing material and photos.

ANNETTE: Why don't you give me some photos and the wallet? [*Keaton hands Annette the photos; she had not yet gone into a trance.*] I am getting goose bumps all over while holding the photos.

KEATON: Here is a map of the area where he lived. [*Keaton hands her the map.*]

ANNETTE [*looking at the map.*]: Something about Snake Creek Road...I get some energy there that belongs to this case. [*Annette is now handling the wallet. She takes her three deep breaths and goes into her trance. Pause.*] Interesting. I got a sharp pain in my left foot on the heel as I started to pick up his photograph. I saw a disturbance in his house. [*She's now getting more goose bumps*] I saw this fellow that Thompson does things with—a friend, I think—Tom James. He looks wiser than this photo indicates. I also saw two other fellows who came in with him, coming into Buddy's house. It's like he had his back to the door, like they pushed open the door. I don't think it was locked, so it was easy to open. I am hearing a lot of conversation, a lot of arguing. These other two men feel very...Mexican, darker skin...One looks like he has long, dark hair, straight, very thick, black and parted in the center...

KEATON: Do these two individuals look like they know Buddy or Tom?

ANNETTE: They have been talking to Tom—some kind of negotiating going on. Maybe dealing with drugs. Yes, definitely with drugs. With Tom, I think. And Buddy has met these two but they're not the big honchos, but he has been talking with them before on a trip. I don't think he went to Mexico but I am getting a border town.

KEATON: Can you hear what's going on at the house?

ANNETTE: Yes, this loud talking, arguing. They're large guys, even for a normal Mexican male—I think they work out. They are getting very upset and very angry. The Mexicans are taking Buddy out of the house. There's a car parked down a hill—yes, down a hill.

KEATON: Is Buddy going willingly?

ANNETTE: Buddy is saying that he wants to talk to the boss— "I don't want to talk to you guys, I want to talk to the boss. I want to get this straightened around." Tom seems to be playing both ends against the middle. It's like he is always on the fence. He wants to be on the right side and not lose. He's really despicable; he is really a slime ball. He has done despicable things in his life. Ugh, I don't like him at all. He is slime; his morals are trash! They are all getting into this car now. The car is fairly wide.

KEATON: Who is driving?

ANNETTE: One of the Mexicans. This is not Tom's car or Buddy's car.

KEATON: Is it forcible?

ANNETTE: Yes, and no. They don't have his hands behind his back or anything like that. They're talking, discussing. Buddy is mad and he's swearing all over the place. There is such a difference between these two to me. Buddy is not a slime ball like Tom. Buddy, if he says he is going to do something, he is going to do it. For a guy who is a big drug dealer, um, he wouldn't rat on his own people. He wouldn't turn his people in. Tom is different—he would.

KEATON: What's the argument about?

ANNETTE: It's about money and the condition of the stuff. It's not the way it's supposed to be—this has happened before. He is really ticked off; he's really angry. He is saying that this has to stop. He can't continue to do things this way unless they pay him...

KEATON: Oh. Is anybody else at the house?

ANNETTE: As you asked me that question, I heard a dog bark. I am not seeing a dog, but I heard it.

KEATON: Can you see the house?

ANNETTE: It seems to be way back off the road. To get to it you have to drive in quite a ways.

KEATON: Anything distinctive about it, anything that would catch your attention to it or at it?

ANNETTE: Yes, I saw something sticking up. I don't know if it's something filled with water. With a stand of some kind.

KEATON: You're drawing a circle with a couple of lines.

ANNETTE: ...I am looking at the house, over on the right hand side...

KEATON: It looks like a silo or a trough or tank?

ANNETTE: Yes, something like that, a water holder, a container of some kind. I also see colors like off-white and gray.

KEATON: As you are looking at the house and structure on the right, where would this car have been parked?

ANNETTE: Like it's down further. I want to go up the road quite a ways and then I see this structure.

KEATON: Annette is drawing a road coming off the main drag. Then she draws something that looks like a tank sitting on a couple of poles.

ANNETTE: Yes, and then the house seems to be just sitting here. I get a lot of browns. It feels woodsy. I feel like he doesn't want anybody to see the house. He doesn't want anyone to see the house from the sky either. It feels camouflaged; I get a lot of trees.

KEATON: And where is the car from the house?

ANNETTE: It's like this road goes quite a ways and then there is another road that crosses. I feel the car was over here. [*Annette drawing as she speaks.*]

KEATON: Was that the main road?

ANNETTE: I don't think so. I don't see any traffic—this place is really remote. It could be a main road, but it feels so remote.

KEATON: You're showing a road that leads down to another road that T-bones at the house. The secondary road is where the car is. Can you see any description of the car?

ANNETTE: I get this dull, gray-looking color and it feels squatty, fat. Like it's an older car, not a snazzy car. We're talking low-key—these guys play real low-key. Because they know if they run around with a snazzy car they're going to be looked at. I get that almost like an interesting paint job; it is not smooth, but rough.

KEATON: Like oxidized?

ANNETTE: Yes, that's it! Feels really rough and looks gray and beat-up. A lot of miles on this car.

KEATON: Where do they sit in this car?

ANNETTE: [*She takes a deep breath.*] Buddy is in the back. He's in between; he's in between Tom and the Mexican.

KEATON: Can you sense anything from Buddy? Is he uncomfortable?

ANNETTE: Yes, he is a little uncomfortable and nervous about...as to why he is in the middle. He was expecting Tom to sit in the front. Tom is behind the driver and Buddy is in the middle.

KEATON: What's being said and done? Does Buddy know where they are going?

ANNETTE: [*Long pause*] He thinks they are going to talk to the boss.

KEATON: Does he know where that is?

ANNETTE: No, no!

KEATON: Does he know the boss's name? Does he know the boss?

ANNETTE: Doesn't remember the name, but has talked to him before.

KEATON: Where?

ANNETTE: In this border town. [*Annette's voice is trailing off a bit; she is speaking slower and she has sunk deeper into her trance.*]

KEATON: How long ago?

ANNETTE: What came to me was four or five months ago.

KEATON: Does Buddy know where the boss is now?

ANNETTE: No.

KEATON: Do you have any idea how long they have been driving?

ANNETTE: [*Long pause, deep breath*] Buddy is getting nervous and he is beginning to sweat. The car is moving and he is asking where they are going. They seem to be heading away from a town. Heading out to nowhere. They're going down this road that he knows. Um, the black-haired guy keeps saying, "Not to worry, the boss is waiting for us."

KEATON: You're perceiving well now what he is sensing and feeling. Is he listening to the conversation?

ANNETTE: Yeah...yes. [*Annette's voice is far off at this point.*] He is very much alive and listening.

KEATON: What's he saying?

ANNETTE: Not too much. The Mexicans have kind of shut up and the driver isn't saying anything. Tom is not saying anything either.

KEATON: They're driving away from town?

ANNETTE: Yes, the road looks kind of twisty. I am getting a little carsick.

KEATON: Buddy is getting carsick?

ANNETTE: Yes, he is really sweating now. He is getting really frightened.

KEATON: Can you tell us what Buddy is wearing?

ANNETTE: Umm...looks like jeans. I am getting a shirt; it looks like it has a pattern on it. Maybe like a small plaid. Looks like it has been washed a lot. Could be flannel or Pendleton wool.

KEATON: How about footwear?

ANNETTE: Oh, boots! Definitely boots, laced up. They look a dark-brown color.

KEATON: Wearing anything on his head?

ANNETTE: [*Pause*] Yeah, interesting that you should ask that. He has two things on his head. He has a hat that looks like it was made of brown leather, pretty worn. Then I saw a bandana around his forehead to keep the sweat off. It looks like he may have been outside before they arrived.

KEATON: Are they back in the car?

ANNETTE: Yes, I don't like what is coming up here.

KEATON: I am sure you don't. Can you see Tom and how he is dressed?

ANNETTE: Yes, it's like Tom has khaki pants on and the hair is tied back, like a ponytail. Something around his neck. I think there may be tattoos or scars at the neck. [*Annette takes a deep breath.*] Ugh, they are driving up a deserted, dirt road. They're going higher and higher—very deserted, no houses at all. [*Annette is breathing heavily now.*] The road bends and it looks like there could be a quarry on the right, not sure…It has like a turnaround at the end of the drive and they are all getting out of the car. There is a deep ravine on the left that goes on and on down. Can't see the bottom…They are pushing Buddy out of the car, as he does not want to get out. [*Annette groans.*] Oh! Tom,—I think Tom is shooting Buddy, and they push his body over the ravine. I can see the body falling and falling down quite a ways…They get back into the car and leave.

KEATON: Will they be able to find Buddy's body?

ANNETTE: Yes, they will find his body.

At this point, the session ended.

The sheriff's department called back after they'd received Annette's tape. They had not yet recovered Buddy's body, but they had Tom, one of Buddy's neighbors, in custody and it sure looked like he was the killer. Annette requested maps. When the maps arrived, Annette put her hands on the maps, got goose bumps, and pointed out an exact spot on the map. She had a sudden flash: The body had been partially eaten by wild animals!

The sheriff ordered a helicopter to search in the area Annette had indicated on the map. Another half-dozen deputies were sent to comb the area on foot. As these deputies approached the area, a couple of hikers informed them they thought they'd seen what could be a body at the bottom of the ravine. The body turned out to be at the dead center of the place Annette had indicated.

When the sheriff called with the news, Keaton asked if the body had the brown leather hat on. The officer said the body had been mauled by a mountain lion or something, but it still had a brown leather hat on.

The sheriff added, "You guys did a great job. Thank you."

A Most Evil Woman

The Jake Thompson case began for Annette on September 23, 1999.

By this time, Annette and Richard Keaton had formed Closure4U Investigations, where they worked together to solve seemingly unsolvable crimes. Thus, in September 1999, they were contacted by Richard Thompson of Huntsville, Alabama, who had seen Annette and Keaton on TV.

Richard Thompson's brother Jake had been murdered in early May in western Pennsylvania. Jake Thompson, age forty-three at the time of his death, was a construction foreman for a new school. When the construction workers arrived for work about

Detective Richard Keaton and Annette.

seven in the morning they found his body in the on-site trailer where he was living. He'd been shot twice at close range. The police determined that the victim had been dead only a short time before his body was discovered.

There were no leads and no suspects.

In the course of this investigation, Annette would come to psychically read the most evil person she had ever encountered. That experience would shake Annette to the very depths of her soul.

Keaton asked the victim's brother to send some personal articles belonging to the victim so that Annette could do her psychometry. The family supplied photos, his wallet, and a newspaper article from four months previous:

BODY OF SLAIN MAN FOUND

The coroner's office said that an Alabama man who was found dead yesterday morning at a local school construction site was a homicide victim.

An autopsy performed yesterday showed that Jake Thompson, forty-three, of Huntsville, Ala., died of gunshot wounds of the head and abdomen. His body was discovered inside a trailer at the construction site.

So that was the total sum of what Annette knew of the crime when she went to work on it.

Annette did the readings at her office in Campbell, California (2,500 miles from the crime scene), with Richard Keaton asking questions to guide her revelations.

The photos sent by the victim's brother showed a smiling Jake Thompson: He was a good-looking, big, broad-shouldered man. Annette and Keaton knew nothing else about him; nothing about his background, any activities he was involved in, his personal relationships, his hobbies, or his associates.

Annette held the photo of Jake Thompson between her hands and said she was already having goose bumps. She took three deep breaths and slid into her trance state and, after a long moment, began:

"Okay, what I am picking up about Jake is that I am starting out with some personality aspects of...I am getting this very male-orientated person. He works very well with men and has a terrific personality. He can get the guys to do things...like he knows how to work with them and he knows how...it's like team work...he must have played sports because I get this strong sense of team effort."

Later, while researching the case, everything I could find out seemed to indicate she was absolutely right about this assessment of Jake Thompson.

Annette said Thompson's sister "could always go to him for help, that he would listen to her problems...that he was always down-to-earth and realistic." Even though Annette couldn't see his hands well in the photo she had been sent, she said he must have had big hands "that could make things and build things," and it "was like he came into the world knowing how to build things." She saw him as a kind and gentle soul, who, she said, "would not hurt a fly." And, she said, he "loved the out-of-doors."

His family described him as a "jovial family man who loved fishing almost as much as he loved his children."

Annette then began to speak of Jake's ex-wife, Peggy Thompson. While she had not seen a photo of this woman, she described her as "smaller, on the thin side." This too, was accurate. Annette said she "was getting tired of dealing with him."

This was to prove to be very true.

Annette said Jake's sister saw his Peggy as conniving, manipulative, and abusive. Annette said Peggy had cheated on Jake [on this point Annette was quite positive]. She said that Jake didn't want a divorce and didn't really understand what had gone wrong. At the time of the split-up, she says, he "might have knocked over a chair and bellowed like a big bear…" but Annette didn't feel he ever hit his wife. All of this was confirmed by the family.

Annette said Jake was "confused and hurt" by his marital problems. She added "there's a lot of money here. She [Peggy] wanted more and more. And I feel that…" she stopped talking for a moment, then suddenly exploded with the word: "Wicked!"

"Wicked?" Keaton asked, obviously puzzled. He had rarely heard Annette say anything like this.

"Yes," Annette said. "And I don't use that word casually, but that's the word that comes to me. She's manipulative and can be extremely sweet and she is just a great actress, I think…that's the whole thing, she is a tremendous actress!"

Keaton asked if Jake loved Peggy.

"Yeah, oh, yeah, he did…I tell you I am not seeing anyone else here in this picture; all I am getting are these two people here…" Then Annette exploded again: "She is the main actor here!"

After a moment, she said: "I am not getting any disturbances from Jake's company—I'm just getting a flat line. There's no energy coming in to tell me to look at anything in the whole work arena that was his life…He was just terrific at what he did. Just terrific! I am not getting any union trouble, I am not getting any other business or contract problems…I keep seeing this female face…all I see is darkness. Her energy is dark. I can't even tell what color her hair is…I get this long face, maybe more heart-shaped face…I see her not really wanting to have much to do with his family. It's like she knew that his family didn't care for her and so she always tried to make some kind of excuse or would be this really sweet, sweet, southern-type female and put on this incredible acting character…acting like everything was hunky-dory and fine and underneath she was seething. There doesn't seem to be a lot of sex in their lives…because he was traveling so much and because she had him confused. His family was concerned about his health during the last two or three years."

Annette went on to describe how horrified his coworkers were at his death—what a shock it was. No one had any idea why anyone would want to kill Jake Thompson, who was so outgoing, likable, and good at his job. She said he was not mixed up in anything criminal and did not have any personality clashes with anyone on or off the job.

And then Annette stiffened up. "I just keep seeing the ex-wife. Oh my God, I am getting my goose bumps again! The ex-wife just keeps coming forward—she's really dark! That's not a good sign…It tells me that she's very involved in what happened to Jake…" Her voice slipped into a lower register and she said: "I feel she's very involved. I feel that this was, ah, professionally done!"

Keaton stared at her. In all their years of working on cases together this was the first time she had ever said this.

Annette was rather stunned herself. She continued: "This is, ah, whew! I am really getting goose bumps again, ah…mmmm…"

Keaton waited.

"She talked to somebody," Annette went on after a moment, then she paused again, concentrating. "Oh, wow!" She sighed heavily. Then her breathing got more breathy and her voice dropped: "This guy is heavy duty!"

She meant he was a professional criminal, a hit man.

Keaton said, "She talked to a guy who was heavy duty?"

Annette concentrated, then, in a softer voice, in a deep, altered state: "Yeah, this heavy-duty guy, he told her he knew someone 'who knew someone who could take care of the situation for her.' Those are the words he said."

Keaton asked her where they were when they were talking.

Annette, still in the deep, altered state, said that they were at a table in a restaurant, a cafe, and the woman was saying about her ex-husband, "He's a no-good son-of-a-bitch," and she wanted to "fix him."

Keaton pressed on, asking her who Peggy was talking to.

Annette said she was getting the feel of silk, "a silk shirt—kind of long-sleeve, off-white, silk shirt. A keystone pattern. The material has a design in it. Very expensive Italian silk."

Keaton asked Annette if she could describe the man.

"He is sitting down and he's got…kind of tan and kind of brown hair, but it has blond in it, like highlights. He is quite tan from the sun. He…ah, has blue eyes…about thirty-eight years old, Caucasian…He's drinking Perrier water—I see a bottle on the table—and he is smoking…a cigarillo, one of those long, skinny…maybe that's what it is, like a cigar…or a European cigarette…Oh, wait! There is a gold chain around his neck. The shirt is open a quarter of the way down, so the center of his chest is showing…He is quite striking."

This, it turned out, was an amazingly accurate description of Andrew C. Daws.

Annette went on to say that they were sitting in ice cream parlor chairs— and they were sitting close enough to the ocean that she could hear the surf.

Then she continued describing the man in the silk shirt. "I see a big, gold ring on his left hand. It's wide and has like, ah…like you have nuggets. It's like gold nuggets on the right, on the top part. And it's a wide band. His hands are very manicured. This man does not do any hard labor…This man is a…he's a…wheeler-dealer. He's involved in all kinds of (nefarious) things."

Again, she was right on the money, as the detectives would later prove.

Annette added that Peggy did not know him well. She thought they were in Miami, but she wasn't sure. "The sun is shining and there are a lot of tall apartment complexes and the weather is lovely."

"But you didn't get any goose bumps on that, though?" Keaton asked.

"No."

Annette, it turned out, might have been wrong concerning the location. They were most probably in Maryland. She was never able to pin down this location exactly. Nor was she able to get a fix on the woman who had introduced Peggy to the hit man. All she knew was that Peggy went to the movies with the woman, and the hit man was this woman's cousin.

When Peggy called this woman back (Annette in her trance heard the phone ring), the woman said, "Oh, were you serious?" And then Peggy screamed at the woman that Jake was not giving her any more money and that she wanted to "fix his wagon" and "get even with him." The other woman said, "If you're really serious about this, I'll have you meet my cousin and he can help you out."

This meeting led directly to the murder.

In a subsequent session, Annette was asked to do a reading of Peggy. She saw the deal being made for the murder and the killer saying, "It'll be quick and clean and no one will know...I'll contact you after...It will be taken care of." And later, Annette saw the man being paid $5,000.

"I don't even want to put my hand on her picture—the dark energy coming out of it is so strong. It just comes right up off the paper. Her stubbornness, her inability to see anybody else's life...Very consumed with herself...self consumed...It reminds me of some of the women who are witches. They become very consumed with themselves and draw in people to their energy field, their web, their cocoon. She definitely did this with Jake. I just see her drawing him in and, ah, convincing him and manipulating him into marrying her...She just snags people in...This is the kind of personality that we are dealing with here."

Annette was getting goose bumps while she was reporting these things about how self-centered the woman was. "She professed to be holy," Annette added, "a good Catholic, but she was in fact a hypocrite and had a lot of abortions...She never uses protection...I see four or five children."

There were, in fact, five.

Annette said that when she ran her hand over the picture of this woman she saw "lots of men" in several places: Texas, Mexico, New York, Florida, and Oklahoma. " The energy is phenomenal! Lie after lie after lie after lie!"

Annette described the woman's energy as hypnotic, "a spell, in witchy terms...She gets in there, into people, and can maneuver around them. It is like a charmed spell that she puts on them so that they become completely fascinated by her, completely taken in by her, completely in love with her, in lust with her—whatever it is that she puts out. She has great power. I don't like using that word, but that is what it is; it's a control factor that she has on other people...If she is not a Scorpio, then she has got to have a lot of scorpion traits."

But then, at the last reading of this murder, Annette did something else she'd never done before: She refused to go on with the reading because she did not want to get into the mind of someone as evil as Peggy Thompson. She flat refused to do it.

She said the woman's energy was too dark, that she was a lost soul. Totally wicked.

There were other problems with the case. Annette could see other people involved whom the police never identified. Annette came up with several names: "Stephanie," "Irene," and "Lopita" were but three of them, but the police could never find any connection with these names to the case. Annette now believes that they were possibly aliases.

Once Annette put the police on the right track, the investigation fanned out from Pennsylvania to Baltimore to Texas. Eventually, as Annette predicted from the start, this case would involve dozens of law enforcement investigators, including the FBI, police agencies of several states, and city and county police agencies. The evidence gathered over three years revealed a case that was so bizarre, the prosecutors said, it almost defied belief. It would result in a federal case in Texas that would lead to the conviction of three defendants—Peggy Thompson, Andrew C. Daws, and another woman, Trudy Moran—for conspiracy to commit the murder of Jake Thompson.

All three were sentenced to long prison terms.

Chapter Ten

Annette Uses the Gift of the White Light for Herself

We had spent a wonderful day learning how to be psychic...We were all standing anxiously awaiting to work with the dowsing rods made especially for her by crystal scientist Marcel Vogel.

"You can use these rods when looking for water, oil, gold, silver, people, whatever you want to find. It is you, not the rods, that is doing the work," Annette told us. "It's as simple as holding the thought in your mind, like water or gold. The rods will turn and point the way for you. Same as the principle of the willow rods bending toward the earth and showing you where to dig for water. Today we are going to use the rods for finding disruptions in the human body."

It was my turn and I was extremely excited to try this new method. Others in the class had been working with the rods and had been uncanny in their diagnoses. We were all amazed at the accuracy in the dowsing rods.

As I started to walk forward, dowsing rods in hand, to see if I could uncover anything, Annette shouted: "Stop! Oh, my God, John, your neck and back are terrible! Your whole back is out of alignment, your right shoulder is in pain, and the whole body is wracked with pain. John, you have so much pain and have had it for so long that you don't even realize that you're in pain! There is a numbness in the body...One of your legs is shorter than the other and that too is throwing the body out of alignment."

I stood there with my mouth open and the others were just staring in awe at Annette's outburst.

> *"John, please, you must get to a chiropractor at once, tomorrow! He will adjust you and you will not believe what a different person you will be," Annette exclaimed.*
>
> *Annette immediately ran into her other office and wrote down the name of a chiropractor that she thought could do the trick.... I don't feel the need to elaborate because everything Annette saw was exactly correct. She was 100 percent correct. It took six months to get my body back into shape and all I can say is that it is true! I feel like a different person! Thank you, Annette Martin.*
>
> —John Brewster

In the late seventies, Annette was under a lot of strain as a corporate wife, entertaining, going to parties, and being a mother of two active teens. She was also a busy psychic doing private readings and teaching, and she was singing. There was a lot of stress in her life. In addition, she and Dick were growing apart. Annette suspected he was having an affair, but she refused to scan him psychically. No matter what, she would not violate this, one of the most important rules she lived by.

Her health started to sour. She had lost a lot of weight. Normally she was a hundred and twenty-five, and now she found herself at a hundred and five. She wasn't sleeping well.

Annette's back and joints were bothering her badly; she found it painful to walk or to swim. She felt exhausted all the time. Her hands were often swollen and red. June and Dick both pressed her to see a doctor and, finally, she went to an orthopedic specialist.

The specialist told her she had a serious case of rheumatoid arthritis of the spine. The doctor showed her the x-rays, which clearly indicated what looked to Annette like little spurs on the spine. The doctor told her grimly that in a few months she'd be in a wheelchair, and there was absolutely no treatment that could help her. All he could do was to give her anti-inflammatories and painkillers. She needed to stay immobile, he said, for the rest of her life. She was not to reach for anything, or bend over. The doctor said that if she took it easy she might delay the transition to a wheelchair for a few months.

Annette shook her head. No, no, no, this was not going to happen to her!

She slid off the examination table and walked toward the door, standing as upright as she could. The doctor called to her to come back; he had to give her a prescription for pain. Annette wouldn't hear of it—she was not going to live the rest of her life immobilized and that was all there was to it. Nor was she going to go through life numbed by drugs.

Dick and the boys were shocked to see her walk into the waiting room as the doctor was calling for her to come back. Annette told her family to come with her: she was getting the hell out of there.

It was odd, she thought later, that what she felt was anger more than anything else. It was as if the doctor had insulted her somehow by simply telling her what his training and his instruments had told him.

When Annette and her family got home she sat them all down and told them what the doctor had said. She told them she did not accept his prognosis and they were not to tell anyone about this—not family members, not friends. She said she would work it out in her own way, though at the moment she did not have the least idea how.

Later, her boys told her they'd never seen her so angry. She was even more angry than she'd been at the Sears company heater installer she'd chased down the street with a knife.

Annette went to bed that night alone and put herself into a trance. She heard Cama's voice: *Use the Gift of the White Light.*

She had never used the White Light for herself. She thought of it as a gift for her to give to others. And the only thing she'd used it for was finding out ailments and problems and seeing the future for other people, and helping to find one murderer (at that time). She had never used it for curing anyone of anything.

Use the Gift of the White Light.

She managed to painfully prop herself up in bed and cover herself with White Light.

Inside the cone of White Light she felt warm and comfortably relaxed. She would heal, she told herself, and she visualized the disease leaving her body like a black ooze pouring out of her.

Over the next few days the pain gradually subsided and she felt stronger and stronger. She took nourishment: just a little soup at first, and then, gradually, more solid meals. Her appetite returned and she began to walk, unsteadily and stiffly at first, and then all the way across the room. At the end of two weeks the swelling was gone, the weakness was gone, and her health had returned.

Another Move

Soon after Annette regained her health, Dick once again changed jobs. He became head of a large division of Memorex Corporation in San Jose and the family moved to a four-bedroom, 3,500-square-foot home in Los Altos Hills, a small suburban city on the San Francisco peninsula.

A couple of times a week, Annette drove the sixty miles or so to Marin County to teach classes at Dr. Jampolsky's Center for Attitudinal Healing and to work with his patients. She was also seeing clients in her home. She was keeping busy.

One morning, about a year after the move, Annette woke up to the voice of her spirit guide, Cama. He said: *Go to downtown Los Altos, park, and walk one block, turn left, walk one block and turn right, and you will find the office you should rent.*

Where was she to park? She had no idea. But she got dressed and got in her car and drove downtown. She heard Cama's voice again: *Park here.*

She followed his directions and came to a two-story building with an ice cream parlor on the first floor. She looked up and someone was putting a sign in the window that read "For Rent." Shazam!

It turned out the man who had put up the sign was an elderly Italian gentleman with a friendly smile and a twinkle in his eye. He and Annette hit it off immediately.

He rented her three lovely rooms, one for a waiting room, one for a secretary, and a large, comfortable room that looked out on a grove of beautiful crepe myrtle trees for her readings. Annette fell in love with the place.

Soon she found a part-time secretary, Pamela, a recent Stanford fine arts graduate who was looking for something to do while she was figuring out what to do with her life. Annette says that she and Pamela were perfect together.

For the first time, Annette had her own place to do readings, and soon business was booming. It felt great—things were definitely looking up.

Annette Meets a Genius Scientist, Finds Two Bodies, Is Assailed by a Witch, and Goes to Mars

Word had gotten around the western and southern suburbs of San Jose that Annette had moved into the area and was a gifted psychic. This was the seventies, and people were beginning to open up to a lot of things lumped under the banner of "New Age." How something as old as being a psychic could be "New Age" has always puzzled Annette. She thought of her profession as being one of the older ones. After all, as far back as the seventh or eighth century B.C., the Oracle at Delphi did for emperors and popes what Annette was doing now.

Anyway, Annette found herself being asked to a lot of parties and she was meeting a lot of interesting people. One of the most interesting was Marcel Vogel. He would later make the dowsing rods for use in Annette's classes.

Marcel Vogel was an odd duck, a scientist without a college degree, yet he held over a hundred patents and had been a leading scientist at IBM in San Jose, California, for twenty-seven years. He worked with phosphors, bio-luminescence, and luminescent paints, and he contributed to the invention of magnetic-disc coatings for computers. He was perhaps the world's leading authority on crystals. He worked extensively with quartz, and he invented the Vogel-cut crystal that had the ability to amplify, convert, and cohere subtle energies. These crystals had all kinds of applications, in industry, in space, in medicine, in espionage...

In 1969 Marcel Vogel gave a course in creativity for engineers at IBM. He had recently read an article in the magazine *Argosy* about the work of polygraph expert Cleve Backster, who claimed that plants reacted to the emotions and thoughts of people. While most mainstream scientists scoffed—after all, plants have no brain or nervous system—Vogel had decided to check it out for himself in his lab. He was able to demonstrate that, yes indeed, plants do respond to human thought. The amazing thing was, the plants responded to human thought no matter how far away from the humans they were: an inch, a mile, or thousands of miles! It was with this discovery, it is said, that Marcel Vogel went through a transformative experience from a purely rational scientist to a mystical one.

Annette liked Vogel immediately upon meeting him. He was a big man, outgoing, jovial, with an infectious sense of humor. He loved to give out hugs. He was not at all the nerdy, narrow type of scientist Annette disliked. She found him engaging and fascinating.

At a dinner party they both happened to attend, Annette was asked to do a reading for a man, Ben Baker, whose wife had been missing with her lady friend for a month. Annette said she was sorry, but no. She explained that she only did such work in cooperation with police departments. Besides, she knew the reading might be gruesome and it would ruin what had so far been a very pleasant evening.

Marcel Vogel took Annette aside and told her that the man was prepared to hear the worst, that it would be far better for him to know than to be held in the perpetual limbo of not knowing. He said that Ben was a close personal friend and that he had brought Ben to the dinner for this purpose. He apologized for springing this on her; he realized he'd made a mistake, but "Please," he said, "as a personal favor…"

Annette looked at Ben: He appeared as if he were about to crumble like a month-old cookie. She said she'd give it a try as long as he promised to take the information to the detective in charge of the case, and he agreed.

Annette sat down, with the party guests surrounding her. She held a picture of the missing woman in her hands, went into a trance, and revealed the fate of the two women.

She saw two men kidnapping the women from a shopping center parking lot early in the evening, threatening them with knives. She saw the men taking the women into the nearby Santa Cruz Mountains. Annette's voice choked as she told of the women's terror when they were raped and their throats were slashed, and she said their bodies were buried in shallow graves.

Annette described the men, their car, the small clearing where it happened, as clearly as if she were seeing a scene from a Technicolor movie.

Everyone at the party appeared stunned. Ben had tears running down his cheeks, but he looked relieved and thanked Annette profusely.

"I'm sorry. I know this must be hard on you," she said. "I can only say what I see."

He said he'd felt all along that his wife was dead and he was glad that Annette could confirm his suspicions.

Someone produced a map of the Santa Cruz Mountains. Annette put an "X" at the spot where she said they'd find the bodies.

The next day, Ben took the map to the police. They were skeptical, but they agreed to take a look. The bodies were found within a few feet of where Annette had put the X on the map. They were mutilated in the way that she said, and they were placed in a grave in the same position that Annette described.

Marcel Vogel was floored. He sent her a letter expressing his thanks and amazement, and he added that this type of work should certainly be used by police departments, a view that Annette had held for some time. He added: "I offer to you, at any time, my help and service to continue to grow and develop in the work you are doing."

Annette thanked him, but said she had no idea how he might help. He went to work on that problem.

As mentioned previously, in his study of plants, Marcel Vogel had learned that there was a subtle energy connected with thought, and that as far as thoughts were concerned, distance did not matter. His experience with Annette had shown him that she was able to read thoughts at a distance from her in time and space. Why then, could she not "see" in her visions what was going on at a great distance—say, on Mars? He believed that she could.

It took a few years, but he was finally able to devise an experiment to test his hypothesis, and he asked Annette if she'd agree to participate. She said she'd be delighted.

On a chilly January evening in 1979, Annette showed up at De Anza College in Cupertino to take part in Marcel Vogel's experiment. This experiment involved a huge quartz crystal that he had scientifically "cleared" of all its energy for her to use to project her consciousness to the planet Mars!

And, to Annette's surprise and horror, there were 300 people in the audience to watch.

Then a weird thing happened. As Annette was being introduced on stage, a woman dressed in a long, black gown appeared in the aisle and let out a blood-curdling scream that seemed to come from the bowels of the earth. She bellowed that Annette should die!

Marcel Vogel collapsed on the stage. Many thought he might have had a stroke, but Annette knew he had but withdrawn into his mind and would be okay as soon as she got rid of this stupid witch.

Annette directed what she calls "gobs" of White Light at her and the woman fled from the theater shrieking. Who she was or why she'd come, Annette never found out.

The audience was in a hubbub. Some thought, perhaps, the witch was part of the show; others thought that the witch was demented and might come back to create more trouble. Annette assured the audience that the witch would not be back, and she said that everyone should just relax, take some deep breaths, and come along with her to Mars.

A few minutes later Marcel Vogel revived and the demonstration continued.

Annette reported later that her thoughts traveled faster that night than she had ever experienced, and she immediately found herself surveying the surface of Mars. She was not agog, the way most people would be, finding their consciousness on Mars. By then Annette was used to finding herself in other places—why not another planet? But it was a marvelous, exciting journey.

She could see mountains and craters, large and small, and deserts, as she glided over the surface. It was like floating in a balloon, she said. There were vast plains pockmarked with meteor hits.

Annette stopped from time to time to feel the substance of the surface—soft and deep, like fine sand. Oddly, she felt buoyant. She said that life—primitive life—had existed there at one time, but it was all gone now. The atmosphere was thin; it was a cold and lonely place.

The audience was transfixed, fascinated.

Marcel Vogel was delighted.

In the years since, various Martian probes have pretty much verified what Annette saw in her vision.

Annette and Dick Go Their Separate Ways

Annette's marriage finally did come apart, and Annette, sick at heart, filed for divorce. After the settlement, Annette bought a small house in the town of Saratoga, near San Jose. For the next few years, she took care of the boys, did her medical intuition readings, worked for various police departments, sang, helped her parents in their hardware store, and tried to get over Dick.

Sometimes Annette Gets It Wrong

It's common in books such as this to create the impression that the psychic is not only amazing, but infallible. Well, this book is different. If I have created the impression that Annette is infallible, I apologize. Annette can be wrong. Not often, but it happens.

As an example, late in 1979, Annette went to New Mexico to give readings at the request of one of her students, Sandy Smith. One of Sandy's friends put Annette and Sandy up at a lovely, spacious home that had a luxurious courtyard with a massive fountain surrounded by desert plants. Annette thought the place was lovely; she had good feelings about it.

Annette's friend had set up a grueling schedule of a reading every half hour. Annette was already tired when the next client, Mrs. Henderson, arrived in mid-afternoon. She was in her late fifties with salt-and-pepper hair, a sophisticated woman, Annette thought, a little stiff, but friendly. Like many people who come for a reading the first time, she seemed a little nervous.

Annette began her reading with the usual three deep breaths, switching on the White Light in her mind. Annette recalls she saw the woman's aura quite easily; it was yellow, meaning good. She began to receive impressions of the woman's health—which was excellent, except for a little arthritis in the back. The woman then asked some trivial personal questions that Annette sensed were evasions; she didn't want to get to the big questions she really wanted to ask.

Annette waited.

After a moment, the woman pulled a photo from her purse, a photo of a man who she said was her husband, Bill. Could Annette say anything about him, his health, future, and their marriage?

Annette put the photo between her palms and closed her eyes. Again she took three deep breaths. She waited for the images to come. But they did not come. No words, no pictures, no feelings, no nothing!

She called out his name: "Bill Henderson." She took three more deep breaths, and waited. Nothing happened. All she saw was blackness.

Finally, she handed the photo back to the woman and said there'd be no charge for the reading. "I just can't seem to lock onto him, Mrs. Henderson. I'm sorry."

The woman asked her if she could try just one more time.

Annette put the photo between her palms, took three really slow, deep breaths, and waited.

Again, nothing came. The only thing she perceived was a black space.

Annette tried to figure it out. She was tired, she thought. It had been a long day. But her powers had never abandoned her like this no matter how tired she was. Strange indeed.

She tried yet again. Rubbing the photo, she took three more slow, deep breaths.

She saw only blackness, all around.

She opened her eyes. She felt frustrated, even agitated. She couldn't believe it was happening. It felt like she'd lost her powers altogether.

"Really, no charge for the reading," she blurted out, and excused herself to go lie down.

The woman seemed shocked, and perhaps a little befuddled. It obviously wasn't what she'd expected to hear.

After a short rest and some orange juice, Annette resumed doing her readings and was relieved to discover that her powers had not deserted her. With the other clients, she did just fine.

After she returned to California, Annette did not forget the woman and the photo of her husband. It plagued her. Would this happen again? Weeks went by and her failure was not repeated, but it was still in the back of her mind. It happened once; it could happen again.

Then one morning she got a call from Santa Fe, New Mexico. It was Mrs. Henderson.

"Do you remember me, Annette?"

"Yes, certainly."

"I'm sorry I haven't called you before this, but when you hear what I have to say, you'll understand. Are you sitting down?"

"I am."

Mrs. Henderson went on, "Do you remember my reading and how you kept repeating my husband's name and saw nothing but black when I asked about his health and future?"

"Of course, I was greatly distressed."

"Well, two nights after you did the reading, my husband, a doctor and director of a hospital, dropped dead while walking down the hallway!"

Annette felt sorry for the woman for her loss, but at the same time she was relieved. Her powers had not failed her—she simply had not correctly interpreted the blackness she was seeing.

"Please accept my condolences," she said. "What a terrible shock it must have been. I'm so sorry; I made a mistake."

"No, no, Annette. Please. I don't think I could have survived if I had known before it occurred. How could I have lived those few days knowing what was going to happen?"

Annette thanked her for letting her know.

Annette Gets It Wrong Again

Well, okay, in the previous section, Annette was wrong, but she wasn't really wrong. But in this next case, she was really wrong. Really, really wrong.

In July 1980, Captain Ben Dixon, who served on a large northern California city police department, came to see her. He had with him the photo of a missing girl, Joan Kessel, age seventeen, of Walnut Creek. She'd last been seen at a dance at a high school in Folsom, California, three weeks before.

Captain Dixon was a skeptic. He admitted he only came to see Annette at the request of the missing girl's mother, who was frantic, not knowing what had happened to her daughter.

Annette put her hands on the photo of the girl that the captain had brought and started seeing images: a lake, bushes, a dead girl with blond hair, her head bashed in on the right side. She said there were no drugs or alcohol, and no gun or knife. The girl had not been raped.

Annette took a pencil out and sketched a lake, marking the spot where the girl's body was to be found. The captain looked at the picture she had drawn and blinked. "That's Natoma Lake," he said matter-of-factly. "We already checked it."

"Better check again."

"I will, but I know nothing's there."

Before going to the lake, he called the county sheriff's department, which had jurisdiction at the lake, to see if they had reported anything going on up there. What do you know, they had found the body of a blond young woman exactly where Annette said the body would be found!

The captain took the girl's stunned mother, Mrs. Kessel, to the morgue to identify the body of her daughter—only it wasn't her daughter! The police had tentatively identified her as another missing girl, Gail Susan Dobson, twenty-one, of Crocket, California.

Joan Kessel called her mother a few weeks later. She had run off to Las Vegas with a guy on a motorcycle who had dumped her and she wanted to come home.

Captain Dixon came back to tell Annette that even though she had gotten it wrong, she got it right. She'd made a believer out of him.

But Annette was left wondering what went wrong—she had the wrong victim in the grave. Hmmm. She never found out. Cama, her spirit guide, wouldn't say. Maybe it was his little joke.

Annette Meets Yet Another Eccentric Genius

In 1979, Annette was invited to Maui, Hawaii, to lecture on psychic medical diagnosing. A year later she was invited back to attend a monumental holistic conference where the iconoclastic Buckminster Fuller was to be the keynote speaker.

Annette had heard of him and was keenly interested in whatever he had to say. He had recently stirred up quite a controversy with the following:

> *For the first time in history it is now possible to take care of everybody at a higher standard of living than any have ever known. Only ten years ago the "more with less" technology reached the point where this could be done. All humanity now has the option to become enduringly successful.*

He had truckloads of scorn dumped on him for that comment. But he just shrugged it off. He was looking at the economic production numbers and that's what the numbers told him.

So Buckminster Fuller was obviously an unapologetic optimist, besides being a visionary, and Annette couldn't wait to meet him.

By the time Annette met him, he was in his eighties, known best for his geodesic domes, the lightest, strongest, most cost-effective building design ever created. According to the U.S. Marine Corps, the geodesic dome was "the first basic improvement in mobile military shelter in 2,600 years."

Buckminster Fuller was an architect, inventor, mathematician, engineer, and something of a poet. New ideas and inventions percolated out of him. During his lifetime he was awarded twenty-five U.S. patents and he authored twenty-eight books. He received forty-seven honorary doctorates from major universities, and was awarded the Gold Medal of the American Institute of Architects and the Gold Medal of the Royal Institute of British Architects. He had one main goal in life, he said: the development of what he called "comprehensive anticipatory design science." This was the science of anticipating and providing solutions to humanity's problems through technology.

He was in the tradition of great American geniuses such as Benjamin Franklin, Thomas Edison, and Alexander Graham Bell, men who were far more interested in the practical than the theoretical.

Annette was fascinated by the man, and she was swept away by his ebullient, optimistic keynote speech at the conference in Hawaii. He spoke of how mankind must care for Mother Earth, and how Earth was a spaceship, and how we were all passengers on her, dependent on each other for our survival. He believed there was plenty of food and resources to go around for all the passengers on the spaceship, as long as we took care of the ship and applied sound technology and wise allocation to the use of resources. He presented a vision of the future of global prosperity and cooperation.

At the time there were plenty of doomsayers around predicting that pollution, overpopulation, and the nuclear arms race were going to doom the planet. Here was a man widely thought of as a genius who was saying just the opposite, and who had the facts and figures to back up his futuristic vision.

Later, at a cocktail party for the participants at the conference, Buckminster Fuller was surrounded by admirers, but then he spotted Annette and quickly motioned for her to join him.

All her life, Annette has been awed by men of genius and drawn to them. Marcel Vogel was but one of them. Her husband Dick was a genius, and so was her second husband, Bruce, whom she would not meet for six more years. And others.

Often, these men of genius found Annette just as fascinating as she found them. Annette is mystified as to why they're interested in her, as if her astounding talent is not worth any interest from these great minds.

But it is the great minds who are not bothered by the fact that smaller minds dismiss her abilities as impossible. From the moment he met her, Buckminster Fuller wanted to know all about Annette: who she was, where she came from, how and when did she find out she had this wonderful psychic ability, and so on.

At first, Annette was so dazzled by his interest in her that she was tongue-tied, but she soon got over that. He invited her to join him and some friends for dinner, and during dinner he was completely focused on her. He was trying to find out what was the nature of psychic energy, trying to define the laws such energy obeyed. He had a twinkle in his eye, told jokes, and oozed charm, but underneath the jokes and good times, Annette could see he was enormously curious about her work.

He tried to put Annette's theory of energies, auras, psychokenesis, and the like into scientific terms, such as the subatomic physics and unified field theory and vibrations caused by eddies in the flow of the space-time continuum.

Annette's belief about her powers was simple: Minds generate a psychic energy field; this subtle energy sticks to things like murder weapons and articles of victims' clothing—and rocks, walls, virtually anything. During times of high emotion, this energy is greatly amplified. Annette's mind is somehow a receiver that allows her to tap into that energy. She has trained others to do it, too. She believes everyone could have the power if they'd learn to use it. Just as Marcel Vogel had done.

That night, and over the next five or six years that they were in contact, Annette and "Bucky"—as his friends called him—discovered that they had an incredible amount in common philosophically, and they shared a remarkably common world view. One of the things she came to love about the man most was his interest in what she thought about things outside of her calling as a psychic, and soon they discovered they both had a deep concern about the loss and value of intuition and imagination in Western civilization, as a whole, and American civilization, in particular. They both believed strongly that the continued development of Western civilization demanded that the culture turn to the intuitive wisdom of its people, and that the intuitive side of people needed to be nurtured and developed and listened to.

Annette had long been saying that mankind needed its sixth sense more than ever to survive, and Bucky agreed wholeheartedly. Both he and Annette believed that the power of reason was valuable, but it had its limits. The intuitive side of man, they both felt, was limitless.

They were concerned, too, that the power of the crowd inflicted a negative conformity that was overwhelming individual creative potential. The intuitive nail that stuck up was being pounded down by the hammer of conformity.

Bucky saw Annette as one who had to hold on to her unique perspective in the face of a lot of negative emotionalism on the part of the crowd, just as he had had to endure in his lifetime. They were both members of the same tribe, a tribe at war with conventionalism and the dogmas of mainstream science.

Annette was deeply saddened by his death a few years later. It was a rather touching, remarkable death.

Bucky was devoted to his wife, Anne, who had suffered a stroke. When Bucky, at age eighty-seven, visited her in the hospital, the doctors said she was barely hanging on. Bucky said, "She's waiting for me." A few moments later he collapsed and died of a massive heart attack. His daughter reported that Bucky died with a smile on his lips. His wife died thirty-six hours later. Annette had a vision of them, hand in hand, walking through the White Light.

One of the greatest things about Buckminster Fuller, Annette says, was that he was intensely interested in her intellectual development. He wanted to know how having the power of the White Light affected her and how she saw the world and the future.

When saying his good-byes that first night, he looked at her deeply with his clear, cobalt-blue eyes and said, "I want you to promise me one thing, Annette: that you will always continue your work in the psychic field, doing your readings, teaching…wherever your path takes you."

Annette says this made her cry; tears streamed down her face.

When she told me about this, cynical skeptic that I am, I said, "Hell, Annette, this is just some nice old guy saying, 'Keep up the good work,' like you'd say to a kid who just got an 'A' on a spelling test."

This shocked her. "No," she said somewhat hotly, "it may sound like that, but what he was saying was deeper than that. He had a profound understanding of the pain that I have to go through to do a reading of a murder, feeling the pain of the victim, feeling the killer's hate, and the loved one's anguish, and the….Well, he understood how hard it is to always be different than other people, envied by some and hated and feared by others. He was different, too, and he knew how hard it was to keep being different year in and year out, how it feels to be misunderstood."

And that's when I finally got it, the attraction she has for these men of genius who are as different as she is from everyone else.

She promised "Bucky" that night that she would continue her work until her dying day.

Whenever she gets discouraged, whenever she's on the trail of a killer and can't quite find him, she thinks of her friend Bucky. Of all the brilliant men she's known, Buckminster Fuller was perhaps the most brilliant, and he was a man who had faced many obstacles and surmounted them, and whenever she feels discouraged or a little in the dumps, she says, just remembering Bucky gives her the boost of energy to push on.

Chapter Eleven

Annette Among the Stars

Dear Annette,

I've seen you three times, and I want you to know that your accuracy rate is somewhere around 95 percent! I can't get over it! You told me about a man, described him to a tee, and said I would meet him, then not see him, have an up-and-down relationship, and you saw airplanes everywhere; "Crusader Rabbit" is what you called him and you said I would marry him in two years. Some of this you saw before I had even met him! He calls himself "Crusader Rabbit" and the relationship was exactly like you said. We are getting married next November.

You are wonderful. Keep up the fun, light approach to things.

   Love,
   Cynthia Darling

At the dinner with Buckminster Fuller that night in Hawaii she also met Buzz Aldrin, the astronaut who had been one of the first two men to set foot on the moon. He was taken by Annette, and she by him, more or less instantly. They were about the same age, both single…hey, this was perfect, she thought. Shazam! He was handsome, athletic, intense, brilliant, charming. The complete package. With his military command bearing, he seemed, at least on the surface, confident and in control.

They went for a walk on the beach. He seemed just as intrigued by Annette as Buckminster Fuller had been, especially in her ability to predict the future. Perhaps it was because, Annette was to find out later, he was a man with great heroic deeds in the past, and not many plans for the future. In fact, at that time he was at loose ends, bouncing from one invitation to speak to another, with no real agenda.

But to Annette, Buzz was personally engaging if not magnetic, as he was especially to women: They seemed to be always buzzing around him, wanting his autograph. Annette had never been around a celebrity like him before; it was like being caught at a half-price sale at Wal-Mart. He didn't seem to mind and took it in stride, always patient no matter how often he was mobbed.

Annette soon discovered Buzz had a fascinating background. He wasn't just a hot rocket jockey. He had graduated with honors from West Point in 1951, and after graduation he joined the Air Force and flew sixty-six combat missions in Korea. After the war he went back to school, earning a doctorate in astronautics from MIT. He created docking techniques that were used on all subsequent manned space flights. Later, after becoming an astronaut in 1963, he improved astronomical star display techniques. He was, in short, a technological genius.

Over the next few years, Annette and Buzz saw a lot of each other and she grew extremely fond of him. Their friendship blossomed into an exciting romance.

He was a man of almost limitless energy. He was the most athletic man she'd ever known. She soon found herself hiking, jogging, and ski-ing—and sitting in hot tubs, soothing her aching muscles. This was the first time in her life she had ever been really physically active.

So here she was, dating a man much like her ex-husband, Dick: technologically brilliant, creative, charming, and—also like Dick—he was often depressed. Buzz had been an alcoholic before he met Annette, and he was attending Alcoholics Anonymous meetings. Annette went to many meetings with him and heard stories of destroyed lives and broken relationships that made her want to cry.

But unlike the people she sometimes saw in her practice, who had messed-up lives but didn't know they needed to change themselves, these AA people desperately wanted to change. She so admired them for that. Buzz had a sponsor in AA, his mentor of sorts, whom Annette loved. He was a joyful man, one who had achieved his own serenity and was help-ing others achieve theirs.

Buzz, like Dick, was a social animal. Whenever Annette was with him, there were always people around. Often they were celebrities, politicians, and filthy-rich people. Annette wasn't exactly star-struck, but she did like meeting people she'd seen in movies and on TV or read about. It was during a ski trip to Aspen that she met one of the "sweetest, kindest, gentlest, warmest men I ever knew—John Denver."

At that time John Denver was in his thirties and at the height of his popularity as a singer and songwriter. His "Leaving on a Jet Plane" had been an enormous hit for Peter, Paul, and Mary. On his own, he had three albums to his credit, but he finally hit it big with his fourth album, "Poems, Prayers, and Promises." His single "Take me Home, Country Road"

(Left to right) Astronaut Buzz Aldrin, singer/actor John Denver, and Annette.

was the number-three hit on the U.S. charts in the early seventies. He had a straightforward, nostalgic-for-the-simple-country-life style that people loved. By the mid-seventies he was regularly knocking off million-selling records like "I'd Rather Be a Cowboy," "Sunshine on My Shoulder," "I'm Sorry," and the megahit, "Thank God, I'm a Country Boy." He went on to do a lot of TV and even starred in a hit movie, *Oh, God*.

Despite his fame and wealth, Annette was delighted to find that John Denver never got the big head that most popular musicians seem to sprout. He thought of himself as simply incredibly lucky. He often said that he never sat down to write a hit, only a good song that people would like to hear. He cared deeply about the environment and about other people and their feelings.

Due to his allergies, perhaps, he was on the microbiotic diet, a craze at that time. He stayed on it for years and claimed it did him a lot of good.

He had a passion for flying and was a good friend of Buzz Aldrin. Denver dreamed of being the first civilian in space. He tried to get a ride on the space shuttle *Challenger*, the one that was to blow up on January 28, 1986, killing seven crew members.

At the time he met Annette, his personal life had gone into something of a tailspin. He was going through a terrible divorce and custody battle over his daughter.

Although he had a wall covered with gold and platinum albums, a great house, and millions of devoted fans, he was miserable and wanted to know what the future held. His best friend, by chance, was Edgar Boyles, who was Annette's ex-husband's first cousin. Edgar had told him about Annette and the power of the White Light and Denver was anxious to know what she could see in his future. He especially wanted to know if he was going to get to go into outer space.

Annette remembers she did the reading in Edgar's living room at his cabin in Aspen. It was a rustic place, with a big, roaring fire. She remembers sitting in an uncomfortable, hardback chair.

She told Denver he would be seeing a lot of his daughter, and he would get custody eventually—which turned out to be true.

About NASA, she said she didn't see that happening. She saw him flying in something, but it wasn't big like the space shuttle, and she saw this thing, whatever it was, tumbling down and crashing into the ocean—and then everything went black.

He wanted to know what it meant. She said she had no idea. She did not think it would be soon.

That was in December 1982.

On October 12, 1997, Denver was flying a small, experimental plane on a test spin when he lost control and the plane fell into the ocean off Pacific Grove, California, killing him. He was alone in the plane.

Was what Annette saw when she did her reading a vision of his death fifteen years later? She suspects it was, but she's not really certain. the White Light is the realm of the timeless. Fifteen years is but a blink. She wishes now she had given him a strong warning to stay out of little airplanes.

Annette remembers John Denver as a sweet and gentle man who gave many millions much pleasure, and she was devastated when she heard of Denver's death. He was but fifty-three years old.

Annette Moves to Hawaii

In the late seventies, Annette had her own call-in talk radio show, an hour a week, broadcast in Sacramento and Reno on KXRX, for which she received no money. She says it was great fun, although it was like sticking her head into a pencil sharpener, painful, but it sharpened her wits. She was forced to pick up quickly on the callers' vibes and they were limited to one question. It was, she remembers, as intense as a singing performance, only more intimate and focused.

During her visit to Hawaii when she had met Buckminster Fuller and Buzz Aldrin, a Honolulu radio station, KGU, interviewed her on the air, and she did some readings for people who called in. After she was back in California for a week or so, she received a call from the KGU station manager. How would she like to do a daily psychic radio show on KGU?

Impossible, she said. She couldn't leave California. She had her clients, her aging parents, her boys...

No problem, the manager said; she could do it from home.

Shazam! She agreed.

She did it for eighteen months and she loved it. The feedback from Hawaii was tremendous; she was reaching out to thousands and spreading the White Light around the central Pacific Ocean. Letters were pouring in from callers who had experienced Annette's readings and they thought Annette was amazingly accurate.

She was still having a long-distance romance with Buzz Aldrin that ran hot and cold with his moods; she still had her private clients and was enjoying her friends and family, but she was restless, casting around for new challenges. She toyed with the idea of going back to college and finishing her degree. In fact, she applied and was accepted at John F. Kennedy University and was planning to go and obtain a master's degree in psychology.

It was then that the station manager at KGU in Honolulu called again. How would she like to come and live in paradise and be the co-host of the morning show from six to nine, and continue with her one-hour psychic show at noon?

Shazam! again. She'd do it!

Her boys at that time were twenty-two and nineteen, all grown-up.

She shipped her car, her clothes, some books, some furniture, and she took off for Hawaii and a new start.

The Move to Paradise

In Honolulu she rented a two-bedroom apartment in a high-rise, with a view of the beach, the surf, and the vast turquoise sea. For twenty years she'd been living in large houses with full responsibility for two active boys. She'd always had responsibilities, as well, for entertaining business associates, running the house, and so on. Suddenly she was alone in a strange city with a new job, a new apartment, and responsibilities for no one but herself.

It felt great.

She was still doing the psychic call-in show that she'd been doing from her office in California from noon to one, but now she was also doing the regular morning show with cohost Don La Monde. Don La Monde was, Annette says, "a hoot." He'd play the skeptic, as if they were a comedy duo and he was the straight man. "You don't really believe that stuff!" he'd say to her—things like that.

The callers often wanted her to sing. Don would wake people up and have Annette sing "Happy Birthday."

Annette on the air with Don La Mond, KGU Hawaii.

They did guest interviews of people such as dance instructor Arthur Murray and movie stars like Tom Selleck and John Hillerman, who were starring in "Magnum P.I." at the time, which was shot in Hawaii. They interviewed recording stars and, of course, an ex-astronaunt named Buzz Aldrin.

The audience loved Annette and Don, and Annette loved doing the show.

The ratings soared for both KGU's "The Morning Show with Don La Monde and Annette Martin" and "Your Psychic World," her noon-time, psychic call-in show. She was besieged with requests for private readings and for speaking at conventions and conferences held in Honolulu. She also taught evening classes at the University of Hawaii.

Annette's trained singing voice worked well as a radio voice. Soon she was doing commercials. The Oreck vacuum cleaner company hired her for all their radio spots nationwide.

Because of her background in theater, the station asked Annette to review new shows and movies and talk about them on the radio show. She loved that, too. But she missed her family, her friends, and most of all her kids. Scott came to visit for a while, which only made her miss him more when he went back home.

Then Annette's father was struck ill with pneumonia and the doctors feared he might not make it. Annette returned home. Her father did pull through, but he was a changed man. He had always been a pillar of strength and now he seemed weak and vulnerable. He was thin and hollow-cheeked; the fire and his iron will seemed to have left him. He took Annette's hand, gazed at her with his soft, blue eyes, and said he wanted her home to help him with his hardware business, which was in danger of faltering.

Her heart glowed. For the first time in her life she felt truly loved by her father. And wanted and needed.

But she knew her mother, who was, after all these years, still jealous of her, would not want Annette around. And she told her father so.

"She will have to get over it," he said. "I want you here."

She couldn't say no.

She quit her wonderful job in Honolulu and returned to her home in Saratoga, California. She worked for her father in the hardware store and began singing small roles for the San Jose Opera Company and the San Jose Center for the Performing Arts. She did her psychic readings part-time out of her home.

For the first time in Annette's life, her mother seemed to be taking an interest in her psychic work and they were getting along better than they ever had. Annette quickly straightened out the store's record keeping and brought the charge accounts that were way behind up to date.

Soon her father seemed strong again, and he was nearly back to his old self.

When Buzz Aldrin asked her to come along on a skiing holiday in Colorado, she said sure. But the trip did not go well. He was in a foul mood, and when he had an angry exchange with his secretary on the phone, Annette scolded him and told him he shouldn't treat people that way.

Angry words were said by each. Annette fumed. Buzz fumed. They parted without making up. She thought she'd never hear from him again.

He did call her again later, hoping to reconcile, but by that time a reconciliation was not possible. She had met and fallen in love with yet another brilliant engineer, Bruce Pettyjohn.

Hello, I'm Bruce

Annette and Bruce met in the summer of 1985. They were both divorced, and both had grown or nearly-grown children. Bruce had a son and a daughter, Blair and Kristie.

Bruce worked for FMC—Food Machinery Corporation—which, despite its corporate name, manufactured army tanks and Bradley fighting vehicles. He was a research manager in the company's central engineering labs. Like most engineers, he'd worked previously at several places: Hester Electric Forklifts in Portland, Boeing in Seattle, Macromatic Design Products in Chicago. For a while he was a design engineer on cruise missiles, so I guess you could say he is one of the fabled, brilliant "rocket scientists." He's always had side jobs and hobbies to keep his inventive mind active. He had invented industrial timers and other gadgets, and worked on the development of very complex speech recognition software.

Bruce is tall, about six-three or -four, on the thin side, with a ready smile and a pleasing personality. I've gotten to know him pretty well while doing this biography of Annette. He's a quiet, thoughtful person, one who will listen to what you have to say and take you seriously. My wife likes him enormously. I said to him once, if we were both on a jury, a blabbermouth like me would be elected foreman, but they'd vote guilt or innocence the way he'd vote. He's that kind of guy. You can tell he's got brains and sense and he readily puts them to use. He's extremely persuasive.

At the time he met Annette, Bruce was, I think, feeling a little lonely. His divorce—which wasn't his idea—had been final for six months. He'd been married to his high school sweetheart for seventeen years. Now, single again after so many years, he didn't exactly know how to go about finding a new mate. Chatting with a woman in the checkout line of the supermarket, he found out about a singles group that was into hiking and biking and going on weekend outings. They sounded like a nice, friendly bunch, so he thought he'd give them a try.

The group had booked a beach house for the weekend. Bruce signed up.

It turned out the house was on a cliff overlooking Monterey Bay. It was a large, four-bedroom, clapboard house with a massive deck. The hedges needed trimming and the paint was peeling, but the location was great for a weekend at the beach.

Bruce had been out for bike ride in the warm sunshine of a perfect afternoon with a woman he'd been dating. At the moment she was touring at a lighthouse several miles away down the beach with the rest of the group. The only one at the house at the time was Annette, who was sitting on the porch in an ancient, weather-beaten rocker reading a romance novel, looking contented as a cat.

"Hello, I'm Bruce." he said.

"Hello, I'm Annette."

He said he was going down to the beach in a van to bring the group back to the house when the lighthouse tour was over. Would she like to come along?

Annette told me later she wasn't really into this singles social stuff. She'd only come because her friend Carol Holcomb had insisted it would be good for her since her romance with Buzz Aldrin was on the rocks. Her son Scott had insisted she go, too. She suspected he wanted the house for a party, but he claimed that he just had a feeling she should go, that something important was going to happen, something nice.

So she went, but she had in mind she was going to enjoy the house, the beach, and just relax, and here was this tall, handsome, very persuasive guy pressing her to socialize. Oh well, what the hey—she went along.

Annette says the rest of the weekend was delightful. The group cooked together and played volleyball, took hikes, had a lot of just clean fun.

Although Bruce and Annette instantly liked each other, this was no shazam, no lightning bolt of love at this first meeting. He had a date on this trip, so he couldn't spend all his time with Annette. In fact, they both remember that they talked about…computers, which Annette knew nothing about at that time, but the more Bruce told her, the more she realized that her father's business really could use a few. Bruce offered to help her get set up and handed her his card.

The following morning at the hardware store she got a call from Bruce Pettyjohn. Who's that? she wondered. Oh yeah, the tall guy at the beach.

He asked her out for dinner—and to have a look at some sharp computers.

She wasn't dying to go out with him—after all, she still thought of herself as going with Buzz Aldrin. Besides, Bruce had a girlfriend. Annette didn't see herself playing around. One at a time was always her rule. And she certainly wasn't going to date anyone who was in a relationship, none of that romantic-triangle stuff for her.

But that night at dinner, she realized she was liking Bruce a lot; he was different without his girlfriend around. The good news was, she wasn't his girlfriend after all.

Annette decided then to reveal what often stopped friendships and romances early—that she was not only an opera singer and still perform-ing, but that she was a psychic. And that she helped cops track killers, that she could see inside people's bodies and tell what was wrong with them, that she was in regular communication with a dead psychic, Edgar Cayce, and so on. She told him all about the blood and guts and decapitated bodies. This usually did it.

Not with Bruce, it didn't. He was fascinated.

So she thought, by God, I am in trouble—he isn't fazed by this at all.

Then in the middle of the steak fajitas he suddenly said, "I was wondering if I might call you 'Annie?'"

You may recall "Annie" was the name she always wanted to be called when she was a little girl, the secret name she called herself.

Then he said with a smile: "Annie is such a sunny name. Yes, 'Annie Sunshine,' that's you!"

Bruce was definitely riding the right psychic rails. That was the rest of her secret name. Annette was overwhelmed at his insight, which piqued her curiosity even more. She decided she ought to get to know this guy better; he seemed to have psychic abilities himself. So they started dating.

What Bruce told me he was most attracted to in Annette was her "up-front truthfulness." He found that very appealing. He found Annette delightfully naive and trusting once he got to know her. And she was incredibly curious, optimistic, and fun to be around. She was never judgmental. He could tease her and she didn't get mad. She looked at the world with eyes full of awe. He found himself falling madly in love.

Bruce Goes with Annette on a Case

Annette got a call from a police sergeant, Zeb Hammonds, located in Manteca, California. Manteca was then primarily an agricultural town, about an hour south of Sacramento in the great agricultural heartland of California, the Central Valley. Manteca had a population of about 25,000. Sergeant Hammonds had a missing person's case he wanted help with.

Annette wanted to show Bruce what he was getting into and it just so happened that at the moment Detective Richard Keaton, who usually accompanied her, couldn't come along, so she took Bruce. She says now that she was "dying to show him how she did it."

The way Bruce puts it, he was interested in seeing Annette work, but he didn't need to see her do her thing to be convinced she had psychic powers. He knew that already.

The missing man, Tim Hacker, worked on a local ranch and may have been a jockey or horse trainer. He wasn't married. He seemed to have liked his work, had no enemies that anyone knew of, and there was no reason that he should have disappeared.

Annette and Bruce met Sergeant Hammonds in his modest office at the modern police station. He seemed a little uneasy greeting the psychic, but he was polite and pleasant enough. Sitting on top of his desk were the missing man's articles of clothing that Annette had asked for, a photo of the missing man and a map of the area.

As is her custom, Annette explained the process of psychometry to Sergeant Hammonds: how she's able to touch a photo of the missing person or objects belonging to the missing person and then go into a sort of trance and "see" things about the person.

The facts of the case were this: After work on Friday night the subject, Tim Hacker, had gone missing. The police contacted his friends and coworkers, and they checked out the usual places he might have gone. No one reported seeing him. There had been a heavy rain the night he disappeared that wiped out any tracks he or his car might have left.

Police and volunteers had searched the ranch where Hacker worked and a nearby wooded area and found neither him nor any sign of him or his red VW bug. They then searched a wide area with a helicopter and found nothing.

Annette sat down, took a few deep breaths, held the photo in her left palm and put her right palm on top, closed her eyes, and took another three deep breaths.

She saw a narrow river with high weeds along its bank, and she saw a hay stacker—a piece of agricultural equipment that resembles a small crane.

She opened her eyes and asked for a map, nodding toward Bruce, who seemed transfixed with the process.

The sergeant gave her the map. She asked where the hay stacker was. He said he didn't remember a hay stacker.

Annette took the missing man's flannel shirt and held it in her hand, closed her eyes, and took three deep breaths. Then she opened her eyes again.

"I see a barn," she said, "and a bunch of men and some cars. A lot of yelling. Tim is getting punched, hit on the head, knocked down."

"Nobody told us about any fight," the sergeant said. "Neither his family nor coworkers. When did this happen?"

"A few days before he disappeared. He died of a concussion he received in that fight," Annette said. Bruce noticed the goose bumps. She was certain, all right.

The sergeant just shook his head. He didn't believe a word of it.

Annette went on: "You will find him in his car. He had a headache. He wanted to be alone. He drove down by the river and parked in the rain. He had a few drinks and passed out. He slipped into a coma. The car went into the river as the waters rose. You will find it near a hay stacker."

The police resumed their search that day, but the river was still full and running fast, so they couldn't dredge. Bruce and Annette returned home.

Annette had been hoping, since she'd brought Bruce along, that they could get some quick results, but the days dragged on and nothing happened. Bruce wasn't dismayed a bit. He had complete confidence in her, he said.

Finally, after a few weeks, Sergeant Hammonds called. They found the car and Tim Hacker was in it. They found it twenty feet or so from where Annette said it had gone in—right across the river from what she described as a hay stacker—where the swift current had pulled it downstream. What Annette described as a hay stacker was actually an auger, a piece of farm equipment that looks something like a hay stacker.

Bruce teasingly said that she ought to bone up on her farm equipment nomenclature.

Annette could tell, though, that he was impressed. So was Sergeant Hammonds, who thanked Annette for all her help and said they never would have looked in the area where the body was found.

Bruce and Annette were married on April 29, 1990. Annette's former sister-in-law, European opera singer Janis Martin (accompanied by Annette's former father-in-law, Emil Martin, on the organ) sang at the wedding.

The Daily Life of a Psychic

I asked Annette if she ever uses her powers for trivial things. She gave me a grin, and with a twinkle in her eye, she said, "Well, sometimes things slip out."

One time, as an example, when June Rucker was her secretary, Annette says she had a sudden flash and turned to June and said, "I see you're going to Tennessee before the sign of Capricorn is finished. December 27th and 28th. It will be snowing."

June, in her written testimonial about this, remembered shaking her head, staring at Annette with her mouth open, and saying, "But I just came back not more than a month ago and really have no intentions of returning in the near future."

But then on December 20, June received a letter from a lawyer notifying her of her stepfather's death and informing her that she needed to return to Tennessee to settle the estate. She was in Tennessee on the 27th, and it snowed that night.

June also wrote about a time Annette turned to her and described her boyfriend's mother, whom she had never met. Annette said, "This woman has gray hair—very wiry—wears a bright-colored shawl a great deal of the time, has a nice personality, and is very accommodating. Her neck is a little long and her eyes are almond-shaped. You will meet her soon and she will like you."

At this point Annette sketched a face and handed it to June. "Show this to your boyfriend," she said, "and see what he says."

When June showed it to her boyfriend, he said, "Wow! Your employer is awesome!"

He said his mother really did wear a pink-and-yellow, flowered shawl most of the time.

Annette's son Scott told me he asked his mother to come to his class one time to talk about her work. She was deep into her talk when one of Scott's smart-ass classmates interrupted her with a question. He said he wanted to know if she could guess what school activity he was involved in. Without the delay of even a blink, she said, "You're a cheerleader."

And, indeed, he was. He was perhaps, the only male cheerleader in California at the time.

The boy had no more smart-ass questions.

Bruce told me of the time he and Annette were in a restaurant about to order and she started getting jumpy, twitchy, her arms sprouting goose bumps. She leaned over and said, "See that guy over there?"

She indicated a rather nondescript man in his mid-forties. He looked like he was maybe an accountant or mid-level manager for, say, a plumbing fixture company.

"What about him?" Bruce asked.

"He's a hit man."

"Is he going to kill somebody here?"

She shut her eyes for a moment, then opened them. "No, but he's a hired killer—that's what he does for a living. Let's get out of here."

Bruce doesn't argue, he told me, when she has one of her "woo-woo" moments. Especially when goose bumps appear, he doesn't argue. They walked out.

Annette is very good about not doing any reading of friends or relatives unless they ask, but Bruce told me that one time he was between jobs and his prospects were looking none too good. He'd turned down a couple of offers he was sure weren't right, and he was waiting to be called back for a couple of second interviews he thought he'd get—but the phone just wasn't ringing.

Then at breakfast, right out of the blue, Annette said, "You'll get two offers today."

"Not possible," he said, "I haven't had the second interview with anybody."

"Nevertheless, you're getting two offers today."

And he did!

It's one of Annette's rules that she doesn't use the power of the White Light for little things. But one time her son Craig called up and said he'd lost his keys and wanted her to help him find them. Well, if it had been anyone else, she'd probably have said no, but what the hey…

She went into a trance and saw…blue. That's it, nothing but blue. Now what did that mean?

She called Craig and told him that the keys were in something blue or under something blue.

"The sky?" he asked.

She said she didn't think so. They were in a blue box or a blue drawer, something like that.

So he looked and looked and looked all around the house—he knew he had had them when he came home—but couldn't find them. Finally he gave up and got a new set of keys, and we all know what a pain that is.

A week or so later, he took his blue gym bag out of the truck of his car, and guess what he found inside?

Shazam!

Another time a client called Annette and said her brother had had his stereo stolen. Would she try to find the culprits? At the moment, she wasn't busy, and this client was also a good friend, so she said she'd give it a try.

She mailed a sketch of two men to her friend, who turned it over to her brother. He took one look and said, "Hey, I know these guys!"

He reported them to the police and the next day he had his stereo equipment back.

So goes the life of a psychic.

One day Annette was sitting in her office in Los Altos finishing up with a client when a Mrs. Lumas called. She had to see Annette immediately—it was an emergency. Her babies were missing!

"Bring photos of them. I'll see you right away."

When Mrs. Lumas—and Mr. Lumas—showed up ten minutes later, out of breath, Annette showed them in. Missing babies—Annette was terrified she might not be able to find them.

"They've been missing three days," Mrs. Lumas gasped. "You've got to help us!" She was trembling all over.

"You said babies..."

"Horses, actually," her husband said. "Full-grown horses. To my wife, they're her babies."

"Oh, I see," Annette said, with a smile.

"You will help us, won't you?" Mrs. Lumas said.

"I'll try."

"There are six of them. We've scoured the hills looking for them. Not a sign of them anywhere. The gate was still shut; we think they might have been stolen."

Annette asked for the photos. They were beautiful-looking animals: standard breeds, with long manes and tails and shiny coats. She took her deep breaths, held the photos in her hand, tranced out for a moment, and then said, "I know why they left," she said. "And they weren't stolen. They left of their own accord."

"Oh?" said Mrs. Lumas.

"They were unhappy with their situation. The black one with the wavy mane—he's the one who's telling me that he's very upset with you, Mrs. Lumas."

She gaped at Annette, and for the moment, she seemed to have been struck speechless.

"They felt cooped up in that...pen. Your corral is a pen to them."

The husband and wife just stared at each other, then at Annette.

"And besides more room to roam, more freedom of movement, they want more carrots."

The husband turned to the wife and snapped, "I told you, didn't I? We should have let them run around more."

"And the five mares want more attention," Annette said. "From both of you. That's why they jumped the fence."

"I see," said Mr. Lumas. Mrs. Lumas still seemed struck speechless.

Mr. Lumas, head bowed, said, "Can you see where they went? Are they all right?"

"They're fine. One problem though: Another stallion is trying to coax yours into joining his group. He's got at least seven other horses. They are definitely wild horses! I see his nostrils flare as he communicates with them...Oh, oh, your horses are joining with them, and they're heading south into the mountains…" She drew a detailed sketch of the hills and trails and a pond. "It's about fifteen miles south of Los Altos," she said.

The husband stood up. "I know where that is!"

And off they went.

They called the next day. They had recovered their horses exactly as Annette had said, including the black stallion and the herd of wild horses, and they promised to do better for their "babies."

Annette Among the Fairies

I asked Annette if she'd ever seen supernatural creatures, such as demons or devils, and she said she had never seen any malevolent beings other than some humans, but that she had seen fairies once.

I gulped.

She said she was on a paranormal bus expedition of England and Wales with Bruce and a small group of friends. They were stopping at enchanted and haunted places, a sort of parapsychological trip—just for fun—and having a wonderful time.

They were in Wales, traveling one of those twisted, narrow roads through the beautiful, hilly Welsh countryside, filled with sheep pastures. It was a warm and sunny day. They were going to see an old church, eighth- or ninth-century. Everyone was laughing and talking, having a great time, Annette recalls. They had to walk downhill on a narrow path to get to the church. She remembers having an odd feeling that something extraordinary was about to happen so she was the first one off the bus.

As she went down the path, she noticed there was tall, thick foliage on both sides. She was looking for something, but had no idea what it was, and she was getting goose bumps all over her body.

All of a sudden the foliage opened up and there was this little face looking at her. Not a human face.

She remembers thinking she must have gone white, she was so scared. This little person staring at her had wings! A fairy? Was this possible?

The little person said, "Who are you?"

"My name is Annette Martin and I'm on a tour. We're going to see the old church."

And the fairy said, "All right." And the fairy was gone.

Annette says she thought she'd lost her mind for sure. She looked back to see if anyone from her group was following her who might have seen the little creature, but no one was close enough to have seen him.

Annette gathered herself together and continued down the path, really not sure about what she had seen. It might have been a child in a costume or something. No, the face was not a child's face. A little farther down the path she heard giggling. Then, briefly, she saw another one, then another. The foliage would part and she'd see one, then it would go away, one after another, appearing and disappearing.

Then one of them asked her if she was having fun. Were they playing some kind of game with her?

She said "Yes," and added, "I'm really happy to see you."

She remembers being overwhelmed and shocked at the same time. At the church she prayed and thanked God for letting her see the little creatures.

After leaving the church, her group was invited to a nearby house for tea. The lady of the house, Laurie, was an American. Her husband was a telecommuter, who lived there but was employed by an American company. This was a long time before it had become a common business practice. Laurie kept looking at Annette as they were all chatting and having tea and scones and crumpets. This woman did not have a clue that Annette was a psychic. As they were leaving, the woman took Annette aside and asked her if she could drive her up the hill. Annette wanted to walk with the rest of her group, but the woman insisted, took her by the arm, and led her to her car.

Annette figured the woman wanted to talk to her about the fairies.

Once inside the car, the woman didn't start it up. She looked at Annette and said, "I just have this strong feeling I have to talk to you about my children. They are five, seven, and nine."

"I haven't met your children," Annette said.

The woman said they were away for the day, but she was hoping Annette could help her anyway.

Annette said she'd try.

"Well," the woman said. "Sometimes my children disappear for a few hours and when they come back they are soooo happy...I just have this feeling that you would know where the children go."

Of course, Annette knew they were going to play with the fairies, who no doubt had told them not to tell.

Annette smiled, took the woman's hand, and told her she might have a little problem believing it, but the children were going to play with the fairies, who live in the underbrush alongside the path.

The woman gaped at Annette, then started crying, completely overwhelmed.

Annette assured her the fairies were protecting her children and the family and she had absolutely nothing to worry about.

Annette left the beaming woman gratefully relieved.

Annette and the Medicine Man

Another strange episode for Annette began in October of 1985. A young woman artist of mixed Indian/white heritage named Jenni Green came to Annette for an ordinary reading. She was mostly interested in some career choices she had to make, she said. During the reading, Annette was surprised to see the transparent figure of an old Indian man standing behind her. His reed-thin body was wrapped in a beautiful, red Indian blanket and there was a long, white-and-brown eagle feather in his hand. He had shoulder-lengthbraided pigtails, streaked with gray and tied with red rib-bons.

Medicine man Teles Goodmorning of the Tewa Tribe in Taos, New Mexico.

He didn't say his name; he said only that he wanted to speak to them. Annette did not know if she was seeing a ghost, or if the man was alive and projecting his spirit into the room. Usually, Annette says, she knows when she's seeing a ghost, but this time she couldn't tell.

He said, "Tell Jenni that I would like her to come to New Mexico and paint my family. We are all getting old and I want to leave something for my children and grandchildren."

Annette then had a vision of a large painting, a montage of corn, birds, men, women, a dark sky, dazzling stars. She made a crude sketch of these things on a yellow pad for Jenni. Jenni studied it for a moment, then cried, "Oh my God, Annette, these are the things that I keep seeing in my dreams and I just don't know what to do with them—this is the reason I had to see you today!"

Annette took a deep breath and began receiving more images. "You must go to New Mexico soon and there you will meet a woman by the name of 'Nettie.' She will direct you to an old man with pigtails. She says that she is not well and that even though she is a medicine woman herself, she needs some help from me! Her problem is with her eyes; she is having a great difficulty seeing."

"But where in New Mexico do I go?" Jenni asked.

"You will see in your dreams. This woman will come up to you and introduce herself to you. Do not worry, she will find you."

Then the voice of the old man, a deep voice, came out of Annette. It said, "Jenni, I wish you to paint a history of the Native American people. A large painting on a wall that will tell how it really was. This picture is for a museum. All the grandchildren must see their heritage. I know you can do it for us."

Annette came back to herself. "Jenni," she said in her normal voice, "the old man is very intent on you doing these things."

Jenny, sobbing tears of joy, said, "Yes, yes, I will do my very best! I have always known that there was something for me to do that was very special and perhaps this is it."

A few weeks later Jenni called. She said that she'd been doing some research and she'd found a very spiritual people, the Tewa Indians, in Taos, New Mexico. She said she was going to drive there for their festival the following month.

A month later Annette received another call from Jenni. She had found Nettie! Jenni had been standing, she said, in front of a jewelry store window when Nettie came up to her and introduced herself, just as Annette said she would. She said the old man in the vision with the pigtails was Teles Goodmorning, an elder and a medicine man and, indeed, he did want her to paint a picture celebrating Indian life.

When Jenni did the painting that she calls a mandala (a picture used for meditation), she received permission from the chief of the Tewa to include

Annette in it. This painting now hangs in the lobby of the New Mexico State Land Office building in Santa Fe, New Mexico.

Three years later, Annette, Jenni Green, and Bruce went to Taos to attend the San Geronimo Days festival. The Taos Pueblo is the only Native American community designated as a World Heritage Site. It is a national landmark continuously inhabited for over a thousand years. It's a complex of multi-storied, adobe buildings, built as a means of defense.

Jenni had discovered that Teles Goodmorning was actually her uncle, whom she had never met. He looked as he had in Annette's vision: slender, dark, with a little, round face. His nose was off-center. He was then ninety years old and a little bent over. He vigorously conducted all the special ceremonies and carried the special eagle feather that Annette had seen in her vision.

During the ceremonies that evening, there was an Indian friendship dance. Jenni Green suggested that Annette join them. Annette shook her head. She didn't want to be the only white woman dancing; besides, she didn't know how. But then the old man, wrapped in his red blanket, came over to her. Annette remembers that for a moment she felt time froze in place. "May I dance with you?" he requested. She felt her face flush and tears flood her eyes, she was so honored.

Their fingers touched and the drums began.

Annette was amazed to find that he danced like a young man, light as a bubble, hopping on one foot and then the other, even though before the dance he had been walking with a cane. They danced for almost an hour. The dance was circular, the people merging in and out, promoting understanding among people.

Teles Goodmorning abruptly stopped dancing, saying that he was tired and that he wasn't in top shape because he had broken his leg six months before. Annette felt this dance exhilarating and spiritually uplifting. It had truly been a wonderful experience.

The next morning she gave him a gift of assorted feathers from all kinds of exotic birds that she had collected over the years. It turned out that he belonged to the feather clan and feathers had special meaning for his ceremonies. He wept with joy.

Later, as they were having a meal, the old man suddenly said, "We go to the sacred mountain now."

Jenni protested that it was getting late in the day, but Teles insisted, getting quite angry, and Jenni caved in. So off to the mountain they went.

It was about an hour's drive. Jenni drove. Teles was in the front passenger's seat, and Annette and Bruce were in back. Teles suddenly told his niece, Jenni, to just keep driving, then said, "We sleep now."

Bruce fell instantly asleep.

Annette and the old man both went into a meditative state. Annette says they were both there in the same meditation. In the meditative state, he said, "You will help me go to the happy hunting ground."

Annette couldn't believe it. How could he want her, a white woman, to do this?

Teles said that he needed her energy to reach the Light.

"Okay," she said. "I'll do it."

At the moment, she had not the slightest idea exactly what was required. She was terrified that when the moment came she would not be able to perform whatever act he wanted her to perform.

She came out of her trance to find he was looking at her with a big smile on his face. Annette was more than a little distressed. What, she wondered, had she just agreed to do?

About half way up the sacred mountain they stopped at a beautiful Buddhist retreat, surrounded by tall pines. No buildings were in sight. A young man appeared and greeted Teles and then the rest of them and made them welcome. Teles said he'd brought some special friends and wanted to show them the "circle."

Teles took Annette's hand and started up the hill. Annette says, "His energy was just incredible."

He told Annette that this was a sacred place used by all the tribes. Now there were some structures the Buddhists had built, but they were all right, Teles said, because he had blessed them. On top was a geometric dome designed by, Annette was delighted to find, her old friend Buckminster Fuller.

Beyond was the sacred circle—a huge circle of cedars at least a hundred feet in diameter. It overlooked a beautiful valley below. They sat and listened to Teles tell stories of doing ceremonies that brought rain, and then they sat quietly listening to wind whistle through the trees.

Annette was awed, feeling a sense of peace and great spiritual power.

They returned to Taos, and the next day Bruce and Annette flew home. Nothing else was said about helping Teles go to the happy hunting ground.

A year or two went by, then one day, out of the blue, Bruce said, "Let's take a trip to the Grand Canyon."

"Okay," Annette said, "let's do it!" And off they went.

They arrived at the Grand Canyon and were going around the west rim when strange things began to happen. Annette fell ill. It came up on her with extraordinary suddenness. She felt like she had the stomach flu, and she was burning up with fever. They found a motel. Bruce had to help her up the stairs and she managed to get into bed, sweaty, weak, and nauseated. She took a couple of Advils, she remembers, but she felt Mr. Death was about to carry her away.

Then came one of those odd things in the life of a psychic. Bruce said he was going to go to a nearby cafe and get something to eat.

She couldn't believe her ears. "You can't leave me!" she protested.

"You'll be okay, honey, I'll be back," he said, and out the door he went.

Annette was shocked that he'd leave her. This definitely was not like Bruce.

She would have gone after him, but she felt she couldn't move. In a few moments she fell into what she describes as "this coma-like state."

But it was only a coma insofar as she could not move. Inside her head all kinds of things were going on. She saw other-worldly beings— wispy, ephemeral beings glowing with light.

There was no sound whatever. These beings just swirled around and around for what seemed like hours.

Then, Annette says she felt something inside her chest, pulling outwards, and it was painful! Like a tooth being extracted with no novocaine. Only this, whatever it was, was much larger than a tooth. She could not see what it was, nor could she see what was pulling it, but it hurt like hell.

Then, just as suddenly, the pulling and the pain stopped. She came out of the coma-like state, sat up, and felt fine.

At that time she had no clue as to what she had just experienced.

A few moments later Bruce came back, seeming as unaffected by the whole thing as he had been before he left. He said it was late, and suggested Annette just go to sleep for the night. The next day, they continued on with their trip as if nothing had happened.

Sometime after they returned home, Annette got a call from Jenni Green to tell her that her uncle Teles Goodmorning had passed away—at the same time Annette had this strange illness while on the trip.

Somehow, that episode at the Grand Canyon motel must have helped him, Annette thinks, but how, she has no idea.

She says that when Jenni visits her now, Teles Goodmorning is very present in the room.

Mandala/Universal Healing by Jenni Green.

Chapter Twelve

Annette and the Healer

Annette Martin's insight is both gifted and accurate. She gave me insight on how to open up the relationship with my twenty-one-year-old son. I followed her guidance and as a result we are once again best friends and it seemed to occur without conversation or effort. When you hear her information, your heart sings, for it feels the truth of her wisdom.
—Carolyn Blake

Over the past few years Annette has been working from time to time with a healer. I cannot tell you this woman's name, as she already has more work than she can handle and wants no publicity. Annette is very excited by the work she's doing with Ms. X, and I wanted to include an example of her work with the healer in this account of Annette's life. I suggested that perhaps I could sit in and watch a session, but Ms. X said no, that this wouldn't work because my very presence would put energies into the room that might affect her treatment.

Ah, the old skeptic in me was already sending off alarm bells. Talk of mysterious "energies" often does that to me.

It was suggested that I might be a subject myself; then I could really see what it was like. When I told my wife, Liza, about this, she said she'd be happy to try it out. Okay, what the hey.

Liza came back with a most amazing story. She said she went into a room with Annette and Ms. X. The room had a couch, a chair, and a sort of padded table for the client to recline on. It was a pleasant room, she said, windows looking out onto a garden, a bookshelf full of books about alternative medicine, and plaques on the walls.

As the session began, Annette put her palms outward, closed her eyes, and did her usual trance, then opened her eyes and told Liza that she saw a dark shadow on or near her diaphragm.

Shazam!

Liza told Annette that she had had a problem there for several years. Whenever she bent over she felt a sharp pain in that area. At times, it was extremely intense. She complained to her regular M.D., who had an ultrasound test done. The test had revealed nothing and so my wife just put up with the pain and discomfort and did not pursue it further.

Over the next couple hours, Liza was worked upon by the healer, who pushed and poked Liza's midsection and moved her arms and legs around and touched her here and there—it has something to do with Chinese acupressure points—and when Liza left, the pain had gone at last.

Well, okay, the skeptic might say that she had some psychosomatic ailment or the like, or that she only imagined that it was better. You could dream up a lot of rational answers. Or, you could believe, as my wife does, that Annette and the healer healed her when standard medical treatment could not even discern the problem.

Okay, let me tell you what happened when I had my session with Annette and Ms. X.

I went there with little expectation of getting any real benefit out of it personally. I was doing it for this book—you know, as research.

Once the session started, Annette asked me if I had any medical problems and I told her I didn't, which was something of a fib.

I had sleep apnea, which is a life-threatening disorder. Victims of sleep apnea stop breathing while they're sleeping. They suffer all kinds of physical impairment, such as high blood pressure and cardiac arrhythmia. Victims of this disorder don't get proper sleep and suffer severe daytime sleepiness and often fall asleep while driving or operating heavy equipment and are killed. It's a potentially deadly disease; some sufferers stop breathing while asleep and never wake up. Anyway, I knew I'd had it for about five years before I had my session with Annette and Ms. X., but the condition was controlled by sleeping with a positive air pressure machine.

When Annette did my reading, she said nothing about sleep apnea, though she did say that I was running low on oxygen and needed to breathe more deeply. She also said I had a lack of hormone problem and that I needed to take potassium supplements. The healer did her many manipulations with me, all of which were painless, and I went home, but I was not too impressed with the ritual.

A few days later my wife and I were to fly to Greece for a two-week vacation. Whenever I traveled I needed to take along my apnea CPAP (continuous positive air pressure) machine. Most people with apnea can live with it if they use one of these machines. You wear a mask with a hose that goes to the machine. During the night the machine blows air through the tube and keeps your air passage open. Without the machine, I would stop breathing (by actual test in a sleep lab) more than 260 times a night.

In order for my machine to work in Greece, I needed to get special fuses, because Greece is on 220 volts instead of what we have in America, 110. These fuses were not easy to find. I had to run all over town for them, but then I did a really dumb thing. I left them on the dining room table instead of stowing them in my luggage. When I got to Greece I was horrified to find that I didn't have them.

I had two choices. I could leave the American fuses in the machine and take a chance that if a short happened, I might be inhaling smoke because the fuses might not blow, or I could sleep without the machine.

Sleeping without the machine would mean that the next day I would be groggy and irritable. I mulled it over and decided I'd sleep without the machine.

The next morning a strange thing happened. I awoke refreshed, feeling well rested and alert. No grogginess, no irritability. I had a lot of wonderful dreams—something people with apnea don't have.

I didn't understand it, but the next day I didn't look for fuses; instead we toured the Parthenon, which was far more fun. In case you haven't been to Greece, it's really a wonderful place; you can walk in the footsteps of Socrates and St. Paul, and see old palaces that were ruins before Rome was even a cluster of mud huts. You can even go bungee jumping into the Corinth Canal: a real thrill, I'm told. One which I passed up.

So I enjoyed our tour of Greece and slept wonderfully well the whole time. I clearly no longer had apnea.

When I got home I asked Ms. X how she cured the apnea. She gave me a quizzical look and said that what she had done was balance my energies and when your energies are in balance, things like apnea, allergies, asthma, and so on either go away completely, or they are dramatically improved.

These energies have been understood by ancient peoples for thousands of years, she said. She is able to see how these energies that surround one's body are flowing, and if they're not flowing correctly, she can redirect the flow.

I asked her what role Annette plays, since she does not do any of the healing. Ms. X said Annette is able to pinpoint where the problems lie, which usually takes Ms. X several sessions without Annette's guidance. Her experience with Annette has been, she says, spectacular. The results they've been getting are truly amazing and extremely rapid.

I can attest to that.

Annette's Power

Recently the *San Francisco Chronicle* ran a piece on Annette, focusing on her police work, citing some of the cases in this book that she worked on with Richard Keaton. An impressive record, to be sure. Following the piece, the *Chronicle* printed two letters to the editor which pretty much said the same thing: There has never been any scientific proof of the accuracy of psychics, they said, and the *Chronicle*, by printing such an article, was lowering its standards to the level of a cheap tabloid.

It's true that some psychics have been tested under "laboratory" conditions and have been found to have problems predicting what card a subject is holding and so on. I'm not sure Annette would fare very well in such a test, the reason being that her powers are not the powers of a carnival act specializing in mind reading.

Wherever this power of the White Light comes from, it is not to be used to read minds at all. I wouldn't be a bit surprised if Annette was no better at reading these cards than I am, and I'm about as talented at it as a block of wood.

In the past, Annette has foretold the future very badly. She once said in the early seventies that by the year 2000 cities in the United States would have domes over them, and I can guarantee you she was wrong about that. But reading minds and predicting the future is not where her gifts lie. She is a spectacular health intuitive and perhaps an even more spectacular psychic criminologist, and both of these abilities can be—and have been—verified repeatedly.

How does Annette do it?

Somehow she can tap into subtle energies that other people are not aware of. She believes that anyone could do what she can do; in fact, she's trained hundreds of others to, as she puts it, "open up their psychic world." She's written a how-to book on the subject, *Discovering Your Psychic World*, which you can get from your local bookstore, or at Amazon.com.

Now you might say, how come legitimate science doesn't know about these subtle energies? It's because science, when it attempts to study such phenomena, makes some wrong basic assumptions. One assumption it makes is that this energy obeys constant laws. Marcel Vogel, the IBM research engineer who sent Annette's consciousness to Mars, took a stab at it. He claimed this energy was quite different than energies found along the electromagnetic scale. He found that subtle energy did not dissipate over time or over distance, which, if true, is pretty astounding. It means that an intuitive who can read subtle energy could, as an example, read the energy at the ruins in Rome and describe Julius Caesar's assassination on the Ides of March, 44 B.C.

In fact, a TV production company was seriously considering a series featuring Annette going to ancient archeological sites and doing readings of what had happened there. Annette claims even the passage of thousands of years does not diminish the strength of the energies. How amazing is that?

How this energy works is not well understood even by those who use it. Carl Jung, the great Swiss psychiatrist turned mystic, believed that we are all connected by a subtle energy he called the "collective unconscious." He believed that many things we think are just lucky happenstance really happen because of the collective unconscious.

Years ago, when I first read about Jung and his theories about the collective unconscious, I was extremely skeptical. Here's an example of the collective unconscious at work, the part Jung calls "synchronicity":

> *Let's say you need a job and you spend your days walking the streets and answering ads in the paper. You're an experienced clydefram operator and there just seems to be no demand for your skills. After a few weeks, weary of this, you decide the hell with it, you'll take the afternoon*

off, and you go to a movie. There, you see a man in the lobby getting his pocket picked and you rescue the man's wallet and chase off the pickpocket. It turns out that the man whose wallet you saved employs dozens of clydefram operators and one of his guys just quit that morning. You're hired!

Jung would say that this was not a chance happening, but an example of synchronicity at work. He would say if you mediate on it, you'll find that there are many examples from your own life.

You might think of the collective unconscious as an energy field that we're all tapped into and our personal unconscious is sitting on top of it, wired to it. We all know people who are able to tap into their own personal unconscious and do things by "instinct," things that most of us can do only after lots of training. There are natural golfers, as an example, who just seem to be born with a sweet swing; natural poker players who seem to know when to bet and when to fold instinctively; natural musicians who can't read music but have magic fingers that can play any tune after hearing it but once. We don't think of them as being psychic, but, my friend, that's exactly what they are.

As for Annette's skill as a medical intuitive: Your organs, apparently, give off subtle energy. In fact, it has been demonstrated that when people receive organ transplants they begin to have dreams and visions from the organs that they've received. In one case, a murderer was supposedly caught by clues given by the recipient of the murder victim's heart.

Annette can read the subtle energies given off by the organs. The energies from diseased organs differ from the energies given off by healthy ones.

But how does this explain Annette's extraordinary ability to go to a crime scene and get into the mind of both the killer and the victim? Apparently, when in extreme emotional states, people emit a great quantity of subtle energy which remains in the environment for decades, even centuries, perhaps millennia. No one knows how long. Annette has the ability to read these subtle energies much like a tape recorder can read the electro-magnetic energy on a tape.

Why science has no interest in this astounds me.

One of the reasons Annette wanted this book written was to interest some scientist to research the phenomenon. She also hopes it will help make psychic detective work more widely accepted and used.

Annette and Her Mission

Lately, Annette has been featured on a lot of TV shows; these include: "The Insider," with James Van Praagh on CBS; a "Psychic Detective" episode; and many paranormal specials on the networks, including the History Channel, Court TV and cable. In Europe and Japan she's often featured on shows about ghosts and psychics, particularly concerning her work with detectives. Annette has also lately been written about in numerous newspapers and magazines and in recent books, such as *Marvels and Mysteries of the Unexplained* by Karen Farrington; *Ghost Hunting: How to Investigate the Paranormal* by Loyd Auerbach; *Psychic Criminology: A Guide for Using Psychics in Investigations* by Whitney S. Hibbard; *The PK Zone: A Cross-Cultural Review of Psychokinesis (PK)* by Pamela Rae Heath, M.D. Psy.D.; *The Astonishing World Beyond Knowledge—Clairvoyance, Psychic Power, & Prophecy* published by Nihon Bungeisha; and *PSI Development Systems* by Jeffrey Mishlove, Ph.D. She was interviewed on the "Catherine Crier Live" and by Nancy Grace, because Annette was the first psychic ever to take the stand in Superior Court in California in a murder case.

The publicity has brought her a lot of clients, and she's busier than ever finding lost people and animals, doing medical diagnosis, and helping the police.

Annette sees herself as having a mission in life to help people, as I related earlier in this book. Her mission was given to her by her spirit guide, Cama, when she was eleven years old. She has thousands of thank-you letters that claim she has helped someone, and more come in each day. The people who write these letters are thanking her for correctly diagnosing an ailment, for finding a lost loved one, or for helping to identify a vicious killer.

But her service to her fellow human beings does not stop there. She has done far more for others than even she knows.

I'll give you an example.

As I was wrapping up this book, I told Annette about my stepmother who passed away several years ago. I told Annette how we had not gotten along. After my stepmother passed away, I heard from a family friend that she had done something to me at about the time my father died (some ten years before my stepmother) and I had no idea what it could be. I thought perhaps she had kept my grandfather's gold watch that was meant for me, or something like that. Annette suggested that she might contact my stepmother in the spirit world and see what she had to say.

I'd always thought that when you're dead, you go to heaven or hell, and wherever you end up, you're incommunicado. Even though I had seen Annette do many amazing things while reading the condition of people's livers and finding killers, I had not much faith that she could speak to the dead. True, among the many hundreds of letters I'd read in her vast collection, there were many that had remarked about her ability to retrieve information from the dead. I just had not seen it myself.

Annette's son Craig, when I asked him if he ever saw any ghosts or angels hanging around the house, said he had not. But he did say that when his grandmother—Annette's mother—was dying and he had come to visit her in the hospital, he found his mother sitting by her mother's bedside surrounded by a host of ghostly figures. Annette said they were ancestors who had come from the spirit world to comfort his grandmother as she crossed to the other side.

Some of the people who have taken Annette's classes report they have seen (or sensed) the presence of an angel—Annette says he is Saint Michael, who was always watching to make sure she was teaching the students correctly. But I remained skeptical. As a fiction writer, I know how gullible people usually are.

Annette suggested that I meet her at her office on a Saturday morning and to bring a picture of my stepmother, and we'd see what she had to say. Okay, I said, let's give it a shot.

My birth mother had died when I was five and my father and Betty, my stepmother, married a year or so later. Betty was my stepmother for several years, all though grammar school and high school. And mostly we either didn't speak to each other, or we screamed at each other, or we pretended everything was a-okay.

Because I was always waiting for the next explosion, which could come on a moment's notice, I lived a childhood in hell.

You may have the idea from watching movies that when a psychic is acting as a medium, they have a bunch of people sitting around holding hands at a table. There are mysterious knocks and moans and that sort of thing. When Annette conducted a session for me, we were in her office; it was a sunny Saturday morning, and we were not holding hands. She did what she always does, she held the photo of Betty between her palms, closed her eyes, and went into a trance.

What happened next was truly astonishing.

Within a few seconds, Annette said she saw me being beaten by my stepmother with a hard object on my bare behind.

Though I had not thought of it in years, this was probably the most important event of my childhood. I remember she raised welts, and though it hurt like hell, I refused to cry. And at that moment I had sworn that no matter what, I would never stop hating her. I remember standing and glaring at her afterwards, trying to burn her up with the intensity of my stare.

Then Annette said my stepmother was telling her she had a lot of anger then, not just toward me, but toward men in general. That when she was alive on this earth, she hated men.

Pow! I had never known this, but it made total sense. Her father had been a drunken brute and after being raised by him, it is no wonder she came to hate men.

She had had a cold and distant relationship with my dad, who drank, too, but provided well for the family and was never physically abusive.

Before this session, Annette told me about what happens to you after you die. She said that when a person dies, the soul goes to a place flooded with the White Light, sort of a temporary waiting room. There, the newly dead are comforted and counseled by friends and relatives who have gone before. The dead are also counseled by angelic beings of light.

After becoming acclimated to the new situation, the newly dead person moves into another place—the spirit world, as many mediums, psychics, and Teles Goodmorning, the old Indian medicine man, call it. Annette, who still considers herself a Catholic though she seldom goes to Mass, calls it "heaven."

But it is not a heaven of harps and heavenly choirs and streets paved with gold. This heaven is a place, Annette says, of learning, of making spiritual progress. It is a place where the soul, which can now remember countless past lives, will work on spiritual problems which have not been resolved in life on earth, and prepare for the next incarnation.

My stepmother is in this heaven. According to Annette's reading, my stepmother is trying to come to terms with her anger and hatreds, and she feels sorry for the wrongs she committed. And, she is seeking my forgiveness.

Did she keep something my father had meant for me as I had assumed?

Annette says she didn't take anything.

The wrong she did me, her spirit tells Annette, was to bad-mouth me; she tried to isolate me emotionally from my two younger sisters (her daughters), a feat she accomplished exceedingly well.

Now then, do I believe that Annette really contacted my stepmother in the spirit world?

Let's say, I think it's highly likely, though there's no way I could prove it. How else did she know about the paddling? How else did she know that my stepmother hated men? Okay, she might have been reading my mind, even though these memories are dim. Or maybe she's just lucky, or maybe everyone has such a memory. I don't know with absolute scientific certainty, but what I do know is that it seemed very real to me.

And I think that is the way most people feel when Annette does a reading for them. It seems real. However she does it, she's tuned into the right vibrations coming from somewhere.

Annette spent some time years ago working with a psychologist, John Henry Borghi. Annette would do a psychological reading of his patients while sitting in the next room where she could not see the patient. Dr. Borghi would ask, "Is the patient a male or a female? Can you describe them? Why have they come to see us? What are their major problems?" and so on.

Then the doctor would introduce the patient to Annette and she would do her usual reading. Her readings were so accurate the patients would accept everything she said instantly. Annette was tuned into the right vibrations, you see, and this would cause the patient to trust analysis and to open up. Dr. Borghi said that this cut dramatically the time necessary to work with each patient, because the patients did not hide their feelings and stay in denial. He had dramatic success even with patients who had not benefited from therapy before.

Because Annette is so certain of her abilities and has so many correct hits, the client responds by trusting Annette. And this trust leads to many good things. Many people who go to Annette for a reading find treatment for their ailments they may not otherwise have found. Others find comfort in knowing that their loved ones are at peace in the spirit world. Yet others find hope for a better future.

But it's more than just that. Most people who have experienced readings by Annette leave profoundly changed, though they may not know it at the moment. I know I was changed profoundly by the readings Annette has done for me. I believe now that my stepmother does want to make amends for the wrongs she did me in this life, and I have gained much insight into her life and the tortures she must have gone through that twisted her. For the first time, I forgive her, and now I'm beginning to repent the rage and anger I directed at her.

The change though, for most of Annette's clients, is more than just learning to forgive and let go.

What is changed for most people who encounter Annette is their world view; knowing her has certainly changed mine. Annette—who sees and talks to fairies; who can see problems in your organs and your psyche; who has had visits from Michael the Archangel and is in regular communication with the spirit of Edgar Cayce and has a spirit guide who is thousands of years old—the very fact that such a person exists means that there is more to this life and death than what the scientist can see in a microscope. The world itself is more remarkable and has more purpose and meaning than can be grasped by the modern, secular-oriented mind.

In Chapter 3 of *Discovering Your Psychic World*, Annette gives the keys to understanding the sixth sense, the key to unlocking the psychic power in each of us. She says we must love ourselves first, so that we can love others unselfishly. We sense danger coming for our loved ones because we love them; loving is a prerequisite for unlocking the psychic power within.

Then, she says, we must forgive ourselves and begin to see the good in others. We must trust our hunches and intuitive feelings, even if in the beginning we make a few mistakes. We must be alert to the possibilities. Perhaps most important, we must have a strong desire to give to others.

These steps she has outlined for others on the path to discovering their psychic world are the steps that Annette herself has traveled. She has spent her life in loving service to others.

My wish for you, the reader of this book, is that you might know Annette, her life, her work and her mission, and her incredible achievements. By knowing her, perhaps, new worlds will open up to you.

And when they do, may you be touched by the power of the White Light.

Index

About the Author

James N. Frey is the author of nine novels and four internationally acclaimed creative writing manuals: *How To Write a Damn Good Novel; How To Write a Damn Good Novel II: Advanced Techniques for Dramatic Storytelling; The Key;* and *How To Write a Damn Good Mystery. A Long way to Die* was nominated for an Edgar Award, and *Winter of the Wolves* was a Literary Guild selection.